# THE KING DESCRIBES HIS KINGDOM

## A Revolutionary Look
## At Matthew 13
## In Light of Contemporary Times

# THE KING DESCRIBES HIS KINGDOM

## A Revolutionary Look
## At Matthew 13
## In Light of Contemporary Times

Rick C. Howard

Naioth Sound and Publishing
Woodside, California

*The King Describes His Kingdom:*
*A Revolutionary Look at Matthew 13*
*In Light of Contemporary Times*
Published by: Naioth Sound and Publishing
2995 Woodside Road, Suite 400
Woodside, California 94062
ISBN 0-962-8091-9-5

Editorial Consultant: Cynthia Hansen
P. O. Box 866
Broken Arrow, OK 74013

Cover design: Greg Lane, Inspired Graphics
712 Washington Circle
Hartselle, AL 35640

Text Design: Lisa Simpson, Words Unlimited
1423 W. Toledo
Broken Arrow, OK 74012

Printed in the United States of America.

# DEDICATION

M y passion has always been for fresh, fragrant, home-baked bread. Therefore, more than ever, this work is dedicated to the Holy Spirit's faithful conviction and revelation. He is the Guarantor of the new and the old in truth.

# TABLE OF CONTENTS

# ACKNOWLEDGMENTS

I am ever grateful to my typists and editors, Don Stavros, Bryce Self, Rosie Andersen, Jill Mathur, and June Heinrich, as well as to my "word-smith" chief editor, Cynthia Hansen. The cover design by Greg Lane was also a wonderful addition.

# FOREWORD

L ike a "drive-by" shooting, I was hit directly in the heart even before I heard the whizzing "bullet" of truth heading toward its mark. It was an innocent enough setting as a few longtime friends shared a rare moment of fellowship. What amazed me was that no one in the group seemed to notice my inability to converse as I tried desperately to appear "normal." But it was too late for normalcy. I had become the target of revelation so simply profound, I knew I would never walk or talk the same again!

I have known Rick Howard for more than twenty-five years and have a great appreciation for him as a pastor, a teacher, a brother, and an example of what a true Christian is. I have seen him courageously stand in storms that would have toppled many leaders, and I've even been privileged to serve as an elder in his church. No wonder, then, that I cherish even the occasional and often brief conversations we have from time to time when I am in the Bay Area. Listening to this well-read, mature believer, who is known for his open mind and often prophetic revelations, is a delight to any seeker.

It was Rick who shot the bullet without obvious aim. In sharing what he'd recently been preaching, he made this statement: *"Influence has always been the bottom line with God for His people both in Old Testament and New Testament times. How have we influenced the age or society in which we live for the Kingdom of God?"* (ref. p. 28).

Certainly I knew of the Kingdom of God. I had preached about it and often prayed the prayer of Jesus for its furtherance. I had sincerely believed in the Lordship of Jesus Christ all my life. What I *hadn't* realized, and what is revealed in this book, is what God really expected of *me*.

I had grown up on the teaching of the Church, which admonished us to become "fishers of men" and to warn the wicked of their wicked ways (Ezek. 3:17-21). We were encouraged to pray for souls to be saved and to invite unbelievers to special church services that would be focused on their becoming believers.

Our tools consisted of handing out written information about the dangers of not accepting Christ, singing and testifying on street corners, and inviting all who listened to follow us to our church service where they could make commitments to Christ. We made great efforts to add to our attendance and measured our success by those numbers. We built large and attractive buildings in which to meet and established extensive training programs to encourage young people to become missionaries, evangelists, pastors, and prophets. We emphasized the clergy to a great extent, unwittingly implying that all else existed only for its support. Ministers' meetings and believers' conventions grew larger and were held more often than some churches met.

Yet with all this declared success, we had not changed the world, nor had we become good seed for Kingdom growth.

God's people remained in constant need of counseling and of repeated deliverance from bondage. Uncontrolled anger and unforgiveness prevented the expression of love. Self-centered thinking encouraged many divorces and unruly children in homes that consequently were unfit as examples for Kingdom life.

As is common among Christians, we became weary in well-doing as we applied ourselves to please the Church by maintaining its goals and standards while at the same time reaching out to enforce the same standards on others.

Is there an answer to our cry to know the will of God? Can one person truly make a large enough difference as to affect the whole world? Is this life to be one constant war, and if so, where is the abundant life Jesus promised?

In this book, Rick Howard removes the blinders on our spiritual eyes without attacking our well-meaning, although ignorant, attempts of the past; instead, he simply divides the truth rightly. Without fragmenting the parables of Matthew 13, he shows the intent of the Master in allowing revelation to be offered and given according to the willingness and maturity of the recipient.

Sermons on the seed and the sower are common to most believers, and much truth is derived from all interpretations. But if you are ready for a bullet to the heart, you may find a life change you never anticipated when you picked up this book!

*Iverna Tompkins*
*Bible Teacher*
*Iverna Tompkins Ministries*

# FOREWORD

As you read the following pages, I can only pray that your heart will be touched as was mine when I first heard Rick Howard teaching the truth that would later become this book. The passages were so familiar and had been so often taught that I was unprepared for the fresh "word from the Lord" that would grip my heart and seize the souls of so many in the church where I pastor. It was a word that would clarify the mission of our local church and challenge us to newly dedicate ourselves to impact the world that surrounds us.

With the heart of a pastor, the insight of a scholar, and the passion of a prophet, Rick sounds a clarion call for each of us as followers of Jesus to fully believe we have been specifically called and greatly empowered by the Holy Spirit to make a significant difference in our world — the daily realm of our contacts and influence where God has placed us. The practical relevance of the Kingdom of God here and now — the supreme importance of our becoming life-giving, fruit-releasing seed that God sows effectively into His world — can forever change the way we view ourselves and our potential for being mightily used for His glory.

As Rick says, "The issue is influence" — and that influence is meant to further an eternal and all-surpassing Kingdom. As my friend of many years, Rick's influence has profoundly touched my life and ministry and the congregation I serve, but never more so than when I first heard him teach what you will read in this book.

I am excited about what these pages will speak into your heart. Like the scribe of whom Jesus spoke in Matthew 13, Rick Howard has "brought forth out of his treasure things both old and new" (v. 52). I promise that you will better grasp the reason Jesus prayed to His Father that we not be taken out of the world, but sent into the world "...that the world may believe that You sent Me" (John 17:21).

*Allen R. Randolph*
*Trinity Church*
*San Antonio, Texas*

# AUTHOR'S PREFACE

Charles Spurgeon is said to have remarked on more than one occasion that for every one hundred men who were willing to fight for the Bible, only one was willing to *live* by it.[1] That statement seems particularly true regarding the subject of the Kingdom of God. There are countless books, word studies, and theological opinions on this subject, yet so many of them seem destined only to produce argument or to bolster set theological stances.

What exactly was the Kingdom of God in Jesus' teaching? How would our understanding of that teaching affect our lives or our philosophy of ministry? We will ultimately spend some time discussing theories that address these questions. But in truth, that is not our purpose in this small book. Our purpose is simple: to examine a specific series of Jesus' teachings on the subject of God's Kingdom, attempting to apply these teachings to the practical issue of our personal and corporate Christian experience.

If realizing this goal actually matters, and you will have to be the judge of that, something should change in the way you view your life and your divine purpose. But what if you conclude it *doesn't* matter? You could then relegate the words in this book to another rambling set of thoughts bent on challenging your lifestyle. Yet first consider this: *Kingdom thought is meant to change the way we face our generation, our era, and, finally, our personal context on this earth.* And that, it seems to me, matters greatly.

# 1
# DID JESUS ORGANIZE A UNIFIED DISCUSSION ON THE KINGDOM OF GOD?

Although we approach all of Scripture aware of its unique inspiration and overall purpose, we examine certain portions with special trepidation. Such a passage is John 17 — Jesus' high-priestly prayer to the Father, or again the various renderings of His final words on the Cross.

We are all gratefully dependent on the Gospel writers for their personal but inspired accounts of Jesus' life, experience, and teachings. As Christians, we ponder each story and statement, carefully searching for every meaning.

But there are those special cases, such as the so-called Sermon on the Mount, where we linger to know how Jesus actually taught and what it might have been like to sit at His feet and hear one of His sermons. Even there, however, the Gospel writers often tell us that these were only *some* of the things He told the crowds. The writers preface their accounts with words that inform the discerning reader that they selected from a multitude of Jesus' Galilean messages and then constructed a typical order. The writers even varied the content and purpose of the messages they selected.

## Ordered by the Master Himself

It is within this context that Matthew 13 rings with uniquely deliberate authority. *The parables that are told, as well as their order and sequence, are set by the Savior Himself.* Jesus' purpose is definite and unified; even His direction concerning the ones who hear seems radically significant.[2]

The scholar Dean Alford writes as follows:[3]

The seven parables related in this chapter cannot be regarded as a collection made by the evangelist, as related to one subject, the Kingdom of Heaven and its development; *they are clearly indicated by verse 53[4] to have been all spoken on one and the same occasion* and form indeed a complete and glorious whole in their inner and deeper sense.[5]

Similarly, the great G. Campbell Morgan remarks:

The chapter is a set discourse of Jesus and not a collection of truths taken from the Saviour's teaching at different times, and set forth by Matthew as a consecutive discourse.[6]

Now, although others seem unimpressed by this detail, I believe it to be the most important introduction of all!

## 'Already and Not Yet'

Many contemporary scholars have emphasized the nature of the Kingdom of God as being "already and not yet" — a clever and simplified way of dividing the present work of the Kingdom from its ultimate eschatological expectations. As John Bright writes in his satisfying and scholarly work *The Kingdom of God*, "It is a tension between two worlds: between the Kingdom of God victorious over all powers and the Church of God at the mercy of the powers of this earth."[7]

Bright effectively eliminates the false strategies that the institutional church often adopts, such as world conquest, political and social action, or ecumenical organization. In addition, Bright's book should be read for an understanding of the believer's decisions in light of contemporary society.

We need to know how the concept of the Kingdom of God pervades Old and New Testament thinking. It is the background, the context, to almost everything else! For our purpose, I can only presume that your desire is to undertake such valid study as background.

There can also be no doubt that the study of Kingdom principles motivates us to reevaluate true success and expected obedience. In his book *The Upside-Down Kingdom*, Donald B. Kraybill presents a disturbing and radically stated view of how true discipleship lives out a Kingdom understanding.[8]

A true student must always reexamine his prejudice in favor of the provocative serving suggested by Kraybill. These are but two books I recommend for the practical view of context and conviction in this study of God's Kingdom as taught by Jesus during His earthly ministry.

But our study is far less broad and far more concentrated. Did Jesus organize a specific discourse on the nature of the Kingdom of God in the age of the Church? Was He uniquely preparing church leaders for the conditions resulting from the growth of the Kingdom in human society?

We all know the context, since Jesus and others used the expression "Kingdom of God" and "Kingdom of Heaven" eighty times in the Gospels alone. Therefore, knowing what was on Jesus' mind when He used the phrase "the Kingdom of God" is an essential, albeit confusing, topic.

George E. Ladd answers that preeminent question authoritatively:

> For Jesus, the kingdom of God was *the dynamic rule of God* which had invaded history in His own Person and mission to bring men in the present age the blessings of the

messianic age, and *which would manifest itself yet again* at the end of the age to bring this messianic salvation to its consummation. [9]

Can we hear the personal focus in those scholarly words? "To bring men *in the present age* the blessings of the messianic age...." *That phrase should stop us in our place.* The introspective question must be, *Am I bringing men and women IN THIS PRESENT AGE at least the fragrance or the hope of a coming messianic age?* Certainly we have an honest quandary if we wonder whether or not Christians can be so heavenly-minded that they are no earthly good!

When John Bright speaks of the tension between two worlds that Christians experience in their walk with God, he becomes painfully specific:

> It is very like the New Testament tension, but, unlike the New Testament church, *we are not resigned to living in it. We do not like it at all.* We have the feeling that there ought not to be such a tension, that it is not a proper position for a church to be found in. We desperately desire to escape it, for to own that we cannot *violates both our sense of mission as a church and our pride.* But precisely that throws us on the horns of a dilemma. For fundamentally there are but two conceivable avenues of escape: *we can give up all hope and responsibility for this world,* retire from it, and let it go its own suicidal way to perdition; or we can, by aggressive action, conquer it for Christ. [10]

Now, this seems to end on a note of typical, current Kingdom theology: a hopeful, finger-crossing faith confession which is driven more by fantasy than fact. However, let's end Bright's paragraph:

> But neither way is possible. The former would indeed relieve us of tension, but it would be craven cowardice and a flat refusal of the command of Christ. *And as for the latter, we confess that we do not know how. Yet we are driven to continue the effort.* So we cast about among courses of action

tried and found wanting for some course not yet tried, or not sufficiently tried, that might set us on the right path. The cry of the church still goes up. It is not the cry of the New Testament church, "Maranatha — 'Come, Lord' (1 Cor. 16:22; Rev. 22:20), *but a rather frantic what-to-do question.* But it is a legitimate question, and it needs an answer.[11]

Our quandary is easily stated: How do we use the "here and now" to get to the "then and there"? We must know God's program *for* this age in order to willfully and intelligently cooperate with God's purpose for the Church of Jesus Christ *in* this age.

Whatever our ultimate answer, we must begin by stating that the phrase "Kingdom of God" always describes a divine act and not a human accomplishment. Our humility must overwhelm our excitement. The Kingdom of God will *not* be a collection of our accumulated accomplishments as Christians — not even as dedicated Christians!

But must knowledge of that fact leave us immobile? Uninvolved? Feeling rejected?

That dilemma may specifically be answered by Jesus' disclosure in Matthew 13, but our *immediate* answer must be the attitude that communicates, "We are not unimportant, although ultimately we are not imperative."

## The Kingdom —
## Greater Than the Church

An understanding of the Kingdom of God is, in its simplest form, an understanding of the *kingship* of God — in other words, of the fact that He *is* King. Or as G. Campbell Morgan writes, "The fact that He is King and that amid the clash of devilish attack, His throne has never trembled for a moment. That is the old (familiar understanding of) the Kingship of God."[12] Herein is the quandary of ultimate faith: to accept that God is in control.

One writer proposes that Jesus was confronted with two immediate enticements in His early ministry: to rule the world by force, or to embrace institutionalized religion. Kraybill imagines the devil taunting Jesus: "Come on, Jesus, go for it. Bypass the anger of the Pharisees. Forget the poverty and disease. Don't stir up the anger of the rich. Why worry about a cross? Go for it, Jesus. Just parachute in."[13]

Perhaps this is the most difficult issue. Kingdom vision doesn't match up to a specific program of action or ethos; rather, *it introduces us to basic principles that instill in us a settled attitude.* Not unlike Jesus, we face simplified enticements; yet the Kingdom of God is bigger than our parochial plans.

Alexander Maclaren, the great Scottish expositor, writes, "The Kingdom of Heaven is *not* a synonym for the church." Referring to one of Jesus' parables, he writes, "Is it not an anachronism to find the church in the parable at all? No doubt, tares are in the church, and the parable has bearing on this, but its primary lesson seems to be much wider and *to reveal rather the conditions of the growth of the Kingdom in human society.*"[14]

Now, *there* is a phrase to remember: "...the conditions of the growth of the Kingdom in human society." It is amazingly similar to Ladd's phrase: "...to bring men in the present age the blessings of the messianic age."

*So we are already at a strategic place of decision.* We must acknowledge that the Kingdom of God is bigger than the Church and bigger than Israel.

Herein, I believe, lies the basic error of most teaching on this subject. As Morgan writes, "It is not a question of the creation of the Church by the gathering of individuals to Himself, but *rather of the establishment of the Kingdom.*"[15]

Can we embrace such a foundation? It is certainly not territory for the timid! The Kingdom of God is greater than the Church. It is, in fact, greater than Israel. The Church may be the living type of the Kingdom of Heaven. Certainly it is the sacrament of the Kingdom of Heaven. But the Kingdom is greater, larger, more inclusive and far-reaching. Therefore, it is the Kingdom of God that must influence our attitude, develop our strategy, and confirm our influence.

This truth alone prepares us to understand Jesus' single discourse. It alone allows us the freedom of His conclusions — conclusions that are larger, more comprehensive, and more radically demanding than we might accept as the consequences of any other truth found in the Word of God.

# 2 WHEN THE KINGDOM COMES

I n this day and age, there are enough studies and statistics concerning church growth to fill an entire library in themselves. Books document both theories and proposed hypotheses. Conferences abound to teach methods and illustrate success. Everybody seeks an answer. Will the solution to church growth be found in the charismatic personality of a preacher, the location and architecture of a building, or the appeal to a certain need-orientation? Is growth heterogeneous or homogeneous? Do we fly cast or throw the net?

In the last chapter, we quoted G. Campbell Morgan, who said that, in the past, the basic understanding of the Kingdom of God was untroubled by the clash of attacks against God's authority, for it was based on the fact that God is King. That must always be the foundational truth. But the revered English scholar then adds a contemporary application:

> And what is the new? *The application of that eternal verity to the age in which we live*, to personal life, to social life, to natural life. Our business, as we are disciples instructed to the Kingdom, *is to make this application.*[16]

## The Focus of the Kingdom: Influence

With all the rhetoric of conferences about waves and fire, renewals and returns, both the true Christian and the victorious leader know the truth in their hearts: *church growth demands refocus!* In the long run, what really counts is not Sunday attendance. The world outdraws us on this count in the arena of athletics alone. The focus can also never be professional degrees or distinctions. No, the ultimate barometer of our success will always be our *influence.* That will be the true grid of life's values and the necessary true measure of our usefulness.

Influence has always been the bottom line with God for His people both in Old Testament and New Testament times. How have we influenced the age or society in which we live for the Kingdom of God? We are to be *salt* — a preservative, not a condiment. We are to be light that brings healing and direction, not merely an aromatic. But are we set on a hill or buried under a bushel? Are we selectively sprinkled in the world around us, or are we huddled together in a disgusting salt pile?

I believe an often-quoted statement of Jesus (which we will mention again several times) is most appropriately introduced at this juncture. Jesus made the statement during a burning discussion with self-appointed enemies. These adversaries accused Him of having influence with demons due to His demonstrated outward authority over forces of darkness. However, Jesus' response centered on the power by which God's Kingdom operates:

> **"But if I cast out demons with the finger of God, surely the Kingdom of God has come upon you."**
>
> Luke 11:20[17]

Without belaboring the context, the simple truth stated here is a dramatic one. The "finger of God" is a symbol often used for the Holy Spirit. As Luke later writes, *"...God anointed Jesus of Nazareth with the Holy Spirit and with power, who went about doing good and healing all who were oppressed by the devil, for God was with Him"* (Acts 10:38).

I personally believe this was more than just Jesus' defense of His ministry before His detractors. The Kingdom of God comes to people in this present age when a Kingdom son or daughter yields to the influence of the Holy Spirit for the furtherance of God's Kingdom. All Christians continually have the opportunity to use the "finger of God" to change understanding, distribute blessing, and display freedom. This is the way God intends to impact the present age: through the lives and influence of those who have heard and received His Word and who delight to obey it.

## A Present-Day Blessing

Brad H. Young is a contemporary author and a leading Jewish-Israeli scholar on the New Testament. His book *Jesus and His Jewish Parables* is a refreshing, if somewhat controversial, discussion of Gospel parables and what he believes to be their rabbinical counter-parts. But at this point, it is his radical conclusion that applies to our discussion.

In essence, Young maintains that the Kingdom of Heaven theme is not an eschatological concept so much as it is a technical term that Jesus employed "...to speak of God's reign as a present reality among those who have accepted the call to obey the divine will."[18] Thus, we have quoted G. E. Ladd, G. Campbell Morgan, and now Brad Young, all of whom urge us to adopt the same attitude as we begin our study of Matthew 13.

*The Kingdom of God is meant to be a present-age blessing, lived out by Kingdom adherents in the midst of their present-day generation — even when those same contemporaries stand opposed to the King.* This understanding, more than anything else, prepares us to both under-stand and be changed by Jesus' single, unique set discourse in Matthew 13.

# 3 'BYOA' — 'BRING YOUR OWN ATMOSPHERE'

I t had been an extremely revealing week. A storm of criticism and hatred had been gathering around Jesus ever since He had sent out the twelve to witness to the Gospel.

When Jesus' hungry disciples hand-picked grain on the Sabbath, the Pharisees saw their deed and judged them. But the Master countered their protests with divine wisdom, saying, *"...If you had known what this means, 'I desire mercy and not sacrifice,' you would not have condemned the guiltless"* (Matt. 12:7).

## The Gathering Storm

Immediately after that encounter with the Pharisees, Jesus once again offended them — still on the Sabbath but this time in the local synagogue. As the Pharisees once more watched from the sidelines, Jesus healed a man with a withered hand. Struck speechless, the Pharisees immediately went outside to begin discussing how they might destroy Jesus (Matt. 12:10-14).

Meanwhile, Jesus talked to the recipient of the miracle, warning the man not to make Him known. Jesus also significantly quoted Isaiah:

That it might be fulfilled which was spoken by Isaiah the prophet, saying:

"Behold, My Servant whom I have chosen, my Beloved in whom My soul is well pleased! I will put My Spirit upon Him, and He will declare justice to the Gentiles.

"He will not quarrel nor cry out, nor will anyone hear His voice in the streets.

"A bruised reed He will not break, and smoking flax He will not quench, till He sends forth justice to victory;

"And in His name Gentiles will trust."

Matthew 12:17-21

One of the miracles Jesus performed soon after that incident led the Pharisees to accuse Jesus of casting out demons by the authority of Beelzebub. But Jesus answers them here in Matthew's record with the revealing words about the Kingdom of God that we saw earlier in Luke's account:

"But if I cast out demons by the Spirit of God, surely the kingdom of God has come upon you.

"Or how can one enter a strong man's house and plunder his goods, unless he first binds the strong man? And then he will plunder his house.

"He who is not with Me is against Me, and he who does not gather with Me scatters abroad."

Matthew 12:28-30

All this controversy seemed to lead to a family conference. Jesus' mother and His brothers sought an audience with Him, probably to dissuade Him from continuing on a course that seemed headed for a rapidly accelerating confrontation. But when they asked for Jesus, He cried out, *"...Who is My mother and who are My brothers?"* (v. 48).

And He stretched out His hand toward His disciples and said, "Here are My mother and My brothers!

"For whoever does the will of My Father in heaven is My brother and sister and mother."

Matthew 12:49,50

32

## The 'Bookends' of Kingdom Discourse — Criticism and Rejection

Now, this is really important! We have seen that the single discourse of Matthew 13 ends with the words, *"...It came to pass, when Jesus had finished these parables, that He departed from there"* (Matt. 13:53). But *where* did Jesus go when He departed from that place?[19]

Jesus went to His own country and to His family's local synagogue. The townspeople knew of His father's occupation; they also knew His mother's name, as well as those of His five brothers and sisters. But Jesus' neighbors were "offended at Him"; thus, He could not do many mighty works among them because of their unbelief (Matt. 13:54-58).

I cannot begin this Matthew 13 discussion without a fervent hope that you understand the "bookends" of this unrepeated, single discourse of Jesus. Religion is generally hostile toward the truth-seeker, often scheming to use the most personal attack possible against him — a lack of support and understanding from his closest family and friends. How difficult it is for a true Kingdom-seeker to see his loved ones falling in line like wooden soldiers for the cause of religion, willing to be used to attack his already isolated position!

## What Atmosphere Do We Bring In the Search for Truth?

Herein lies an understanding for this book. Every Christian individually brings an atmosphere to the search for truth. For some, that atmosphere becomes an unapproachable barrier that no teacher's word could ever penetrate. Thank God, the opposite can also be true! Some can bring such openness and expectancy that even the poorest presentation bursts into living flames.

Matthew 13 is not a collection arranged by inspired writers. The seven or eight parables in this set discourse of Jesus are arranged in His order, not according to some random selection. *That ought to*

33

*make us sit up and take notice.* Jesus Himself arranged this teaching! But an unreceptive attitude can make even such a pinnacle of truth a point of death to our own grasp of that truth. Our minds can be so prejudiced against the messenger, or perhaps by our own preconceptions of truth, that the message never has a chance.

Around us is an atmosphere we bring. It either serves as a barrier or as an open door of expectancy. It is more often the explanation for the end results produced in our lives than what is said or written. Please believe me on this point, for I have often demonstrated the sad truth of being unable to receive because of my own self-erected barriers. And as you believe me, I will plead for new revelation, as fragrant as freshly baked bread, to break upon your conscience and prepare the way for the entrance of truth.

I know now why one great scholar, in writing on Matthew 13 concerning the Kingdom of God, cried out, "Will not somebody give me another phrase? How shall I find another? There is no better, but we have taken these Bible phrases and robbed them of their virtue by repetition."[20]

# 4 NAÏVE ANSWERS

"**O**n the same day [the day Jesus' intimate family had come prepared to dissuade Him from conflict] *Jesus went out of the house and sat by the sea*" (Matt. 13:1). Like me, like many of us, a time of reflection to review and refresh was necessary even for the Master.

"*And great multitudes were gathered together to Him, so that He got into a boat and sat; and the whole multitude stood on the shore*" (Matt. 13:2). Was this an interruption? Could Jesus find no moment to Himself, even amid these most depressing recent developments? Or was it destiny — an encouraging, prophetic look at future acceptance and an ultimate response from the people He came to reach?

## Truth in the Midst Of the Storm

No matter how Jesus felt about the people's presence that day, His response came from the heart of a true teacher: "*Then He spoke many things to them in parables, saying...*" (v. 3). Here was an obvious outflow of Jesus' life at that moment. It was a sermon from the most vulnerable of His circumstances — a sermon, in truth, from the most intimate context imaginable.

There was indeed a gathering storm on the horizon. The very background of this moment was set against the darkened context of strife. Jesus had seen His disciples' growing confusion within the house before He left to stroll down to the sea. He knew He needed to reassure them that although their labor might seem wasted, they could look forward to future abundant harvest.

What's more, Jesus needed His disciples to understand the true principles of Kingdom methodology and success. They seemed so obviously in conflict with the recent barrage of opposing human thought and program. Yes, present rejection would be met by a promise of future victory, but there were imperative lessons to be learned along the way — a right way to assure harvest, a true understanding of the necessary attitude for Kingdom success.

## The Divine Order
## Of the Parables

Jesus had all this in mind as He set the order of the discourse that followed. First, He spoke four parables to the multitude that gathered about Him on the seashore, including a clear explanation of His first and most fundamental teaching in this sermon. These four parables are foundational in establishing a true philosophy for Kingdom of God strategy.

Jesus showed a special interest in making sure the crowd understood what the "sowing" was all about and how it could be recognized. He was clear as well about His use of parables in general. (This method of teaching had always created controversy but served as a proven way to quickly divide a crowd between the curious and the consequential.)

Then Jesus dismissed the multitude to their journey home. Certainly there was enough in their portion of this sermon for the people to chew on for a lifetime!

After the crowd departed, Jesus reentered the house. From this point on, His teaching was truly for the disciples alone. He knew they were wondering about the tares sown by "an enemy" among the good seed of the sower. Doubtless, their major concern was with the owner's strategy presented to his servants: "Let both grow together until the harvest." But like any good teacher, Jesus awaited *their* question. The answer would mean more when they asked for it!

Jesus then gave His disciples two more quick parables that established the philosophy of Heaven toward mankind. He knew these two parables would really stretch the disciples' mentality, turning them from the attitude of exclusion taught by the religious to the attitude of human value and accessibility that must predominate true Kingdom life.

Finally, Jesus concluded His discourse, now limited to the disciples, with a challenging view of Kingdom attitude during the period between His physical presence and His ultimate establishment of the Kingdom. He explained that the active Kingdom was to be like a "dragnet," gathering indiscriminately and deferring judgment until the end of the age. He again assured the disciples of ultimate eternal judgment, yet argued for an open attitude during the gathering. As with the beginning of this message, this ending was startling, upsetting the basket of "normal" religious concepts.

## A Naïve Response
## To a Profound Query

It is then my view that Jesus presented an eighth parable. Like the eighth note of a piano octave, this parable represented a truly new beginning.

"Have you understood *all* these things?" Jesus asked.

And the disciples responded, "Yes, Lord."

Now, these disciples had just heard the single most explanatory, inclusive view of the Kingdom of God and its operation ever given. The ramifications of this well-planned, single discourse would take a college course — developed according to this divine syllabus — to explore and understand.

What Matthew 13 records is truly revolutionary and instructive, designed to provide clarity for the generations of Kingdom leaders and followers who were yet to come. But when Jesus asked the disciples, "Do you truly understand *all* of this?" their response was immediate and unquestioning: "Yes, Lord."

How naïve! This certainly proves without question that all these disciples were *men*. No woman would have let such phenomenal truths pass by without a "world" of questions! Since I, too, am a man by genetics, I believe the response of these men demands amplification.

A friend once asked me why several million male sperm cells were required to fertilize a single female egg. When I had no answer, he replied, "Because only one in a million men will ask directions!" Although clever enough to deserve a chuckle, this little joke hits uncomfortably close to home for the male gender!

This aversion to admitting ignorance often makes life unnecessarily complicated for the man who refuses to ask. A case in point: A man awoke, showered, and then stumbled to the breakfast table, only to be met by his radiantly happy wife. "I'll bet you don't know what day it is," she said playfully.

Her question and its implied responsibility so shattered the man's awareness that he proclaimed quickly, *"Of course, I do!"* Then he hurried out the door, forgetting even his coffee.

At ten o'clock that same morning, the doorbell rang and the housewife was greeted by a delivery man with a dozen beautiful, long-stemmed roses. She was overjoyed! The doorbell rang again at 1 p.m.; it was a second delivery man, this one holding a foil-wrapped, two-pound box of the wife's favorite chocolates.

The afternoon climaxed with the delivery of a beautiful dress from the wife's favorite boutique. She couldn't wait for her husband to return.

That evening the man walked through the door unafraid, confident that he had fulfilled his marital responsibility in the matter. Imagine his immediate thoughts when his wife gushed, *"Oh, Honey! First the roses, then the chocolates, and finally my gorgeous dress. This has been the most wonderful Groundhog Day of my life!"*

Indeed! A single question can often clear up a world of misunderstanding!

But after asking His startling question, Jesus didn't criticize or upbraid His disciples for their reply. He didn't ask, "Who are you kidding?" Neither did He offer sarcasm or denial — only a parable that should bring us all to our knees.

Jesus simply replied, *"...Therefore every scribe instructed concerning the kingdom of heaven is like a householder who brings out of his treasure things new and old"* (Matt. 13:52).

*What a simple but spectacular hope is contained in that sentence!* How it eloquently summarizes and applies Jesus' discourse to a glorious possibility!

Eugene Peterson in *The Message* translates these words as follows:

> Jesus asked, "Are you starting to get a handle on all this?"
> They answered, "Yes."
> He said, "Then you see how every student well-trained in God's kingdom is like the owner of a general store who can put his hands on anything you need, old or new, exactly when you need it."
>
> Matthew 13:51,52[21]

Do you shudder when you hear these words? Do you move to the edge of your seat? Does Jesus' response to His disciples here provide you with a whole new level of interest to study this particular teaching?

## Laying Hold of the Answers
## For Your Generation

The scribes of biblical times knew the answer when wise men inquired of Herod the way to the newborn King. In Jewish society, every man longed to have the time to study and know the Scriptures. Jesus therefore used the scribe as a model to underline a specific purpose to His teaching.

In essence, Jesus was saying, "In this teaching are contained the answers for the questions that follow. If you can grasp these truths, you will ultimately lay your hand on the answer for each era and every generation. You will know when to bring forth the *old, unchanging realities* and when to make the *new, specific applications*."

David, it is said, "served his generation."[22] Although he adhered to unchanging biblical awareness and foundations, David knew how to lay his hand on what was needed in his contemporary moment. Surely that must be our desire as well — to continually provide our present age with relevant, timeless truth, interpreted to immediate and necessary application.

What had Jesus said in the foregoing teaching that would merit this unprecedented promise? *What must we know of all these things that would bind us to such a promise?* That must be the purpose of our search and the outline of this book. May we ultimately in truth and not naivete say to our Lord, "Yes, Lord. I understand all these things."

# 5 THE POTENTIAL OF PARABLES

lthough we believe that Matthew 13 is a single discourse taught by Jesus in one specific setting, the chapter is interspersed with important commentary sections as well. For example, after Jesus finishes presenting the first four parables to the multitude and begins His trek toward a house where He can teach His disciples exclusively, Matthew adds an explanatory note:

> **All these things Jesus spoke to the multitude in parables; and without a parable He did not speak to them,**
>
> **that it might be fulfilled which was spoken by the prophet, saying: "I will open My mouth in parables; I will utter things kept secret from the foundation of the world."** [23]
>
> Matthew 13:34,35

What are parables and why did Jesus use them? That specific discussion actually occupies as much space as the longest parable in one study. Answering that question, therefore, demands our priority attention.

## Parables as a Method of Teaching

The Greek word in the original scriptures is *parabole*, which could literally be translated *a throwing down* or *placing of things side*

41

*by side.* It also carries the meaning of *a comparison* or *the putting of one thing beside another to make a point.*

Jesus' parables were mostly short stories, drawn from the everyday life of His hearers to enlighten them about the specific truths He urgently desired to convey. It has been said that a parable is an *earthly* story with a *heavenly* meaning.

Robert Farrar Capon writes, "On its face it refers to the simple teaching device that Jesus so often transformed into something that mystified more than it informed."[24] Whether or not you agree with that, the parables of Jesus did produce a controversial and divisive reaction. The Guidepost's *Home Bible Study Program* simplifies the conclusion by saying, "The honest and sincere person caught the meaning of His stories, *but the merely curious or critical usually missed the point.*"[25]

Certainly there was the sense of a hidden message in Jesus' parables. He worded them carefully, it would seem, to avoid offending those who were hostile or unprepared to receive truth.

*I believe parables were always given in grace to meet the need of near-sightedness.* The parable is always a method of God's infinite love. Yet as we shall see, parables *do* reveal the condition of the heart. It is impossible for a person with a wrong spirit to receive the truth of a parable.

## The Purpose Behind Jesus' Parables

After Jesus' first parable in this specific and carefully arranged teaching, the disciples asked, "Why do you speak to them in parables?" The Master's answer demands a careful study in itself, which would be another book. Here, however, we must at least note the purpose of His method.

> He answered and said to them, "Because it has been given to you to know the mysteries of the kingdom of heaven, but to them it has not been given.

"For whoever has, to him more will be given, and he will
have abundance; but whoever does not have, even what he has
will be taken away from him.

"Therefore I speak to them in parables, because seeing they
do not see, and hearing they do not hear, nor do they understand."

Matthew 13:11-13

So there are mysteries to the Kingdom of God that demand
understanding. God expects us to carefully place each new understanding He gives us upon the ones previously understood. That
should sound familiar to us, for it is a standard principle. We cannot
advance in math, physics, English, or Latin if we have failed to first
receive and understand the fundamental truths of the subject at
hand.

It seems that the context of Jesus' response to the disciples'
question places special emphasis on *this* series of parables, especially
on the necessity of receiving with understanding this first parable of
the sower. But is Jesus actually saying that this parable is meant to
produce blindness in some, giving them no chance to receive truth?
Is a person's ability to understand the principles of divine wisdom
simply in the throw of the dice?

I don't think so. Read on as Jesus continues:

"And in them the prophecy of Isaiah is fulfilled, which says:
'Hearing you will hear and shall not understand, and seeing you
will see and not perceive;

'For the hearts of this people have grown dull. Their ears are
hard of hearing, and their eyes they have closed, lest they should
see with their eyes and hear with their ears, lest they should
understand with their hearts and turn, so that I should heal
them.'"

Matthew 13:14,15[26]

In the Old Testament text, the blindness is clearly a result of
previous action. *The people caused themselves not to hear or see.* They
produced in themselves the dullness of incomprehension.

Let us neither belabor this point nor ignore its significance. If the parable is a method of infinite love, it cannot at the same time be designed to produce blindness. The people had *allowed* their eyes not to see and had specifically *hardened their hearts*. The action described is in the past tense, denoting a prior decision.

Yet even here, as always, Jesus must press home the positive — the potential.

> "But blessed are your eyes for they see, and your ears for they hear;
>
> "for assuredly, I say to you that many prophets and righteous men desired to see what you see, and did not see it, and to hear what you hear, and did not hear it.
>
> Matthew 13:16,17

Parallel to these words are several passages in which we are told that prophets and even angels could see only in a glass darkly until the Son of Man was revealed in fulfillment of the promise. *Truth accepted leads to hope realized*, even when time and detail remain unrevealed.

## Greater Understanding — Or Greater Condemnation

We see again the power of the parable — the continuation of understanding in the light of later fulfillment. No wonder the *Message* translation of Jesus' words in these verses almost shouts!

> "But you have God-blessed eyes — eyes that see! And God-blessed ears — ears that hear! A lot of people, prophets and humble believers among them, would have given anything to see what you are seeing, to hear what you are hearing, but never had the chance."
>
> Matthew 13:16,17[27]

Here then is the divine potential of parables: understanding to the sincere and honest hearer, but even more condemnation and darkness to those who are critical and unhearing — to those who have previously darkened their own hearts, their own eyes and ears.

I am reminded here of the comment of G. K. Chesterton, satirist and critic, who wrote that if you give people an analogy they claim to not understand, you should graciously offer them another. "If they say they don't understand that either, you should *oblige them with a third.*"

But from that point on, Chesterton suggests a change of tactic: "If they still insist they do not understand, *the only thing left is to praise them for the one truth they do have a grip on. 'Yes,' you tell them, 'that is quite correct. You do NOT understand.'"*[28]

# 6   SEED OR SOIL?

Perhaps it seems like presumption to restate what has become a theme for this book. *It is possible for the Christian to know God's program and to both willfully and intelligently cooperate with that purpose for the Church of Jesus Christ in this age.* The very nature of Matthew 13 makes this discussion important. This is clearly *not* a collection of truths taken from the Savior's teaching at different times and then set forth by an inspired writer as a consecutive discourse.

We stress again: *Jesus Himself set this discourse.* He ordered the material and, in the case of the two foundational parables, Himself interpreted their meaning as well. No evangelist, however reverently, compiled a collection of Jesus' sermons, all related to one subject: the Kingdom of Heaven and its development.

Is there another place in Scripture like this? Certainly the writers who present the so-called Sermon on the Mount begin their coverage by expressing that the following truths were the kinds of divine principles Jesus was teaching throughout the Galilean villages (Matt. 4:23). Whether or not there are other set discussions, Matthew 13 must nevertheless stand in a unique and irreplaceable category. We should approach its sacred truths with a "shoes off" reverence to what we hear and a holy supplication that we would receive clearly through God-blessed ears and eyes. This is indeed holy ground.

## One Parable —
## Two Applications?

Jesus begins His discourse with a story we have heard from Him before, one that is familiar and extremely applicable to His hearers. It's about agriculture, about sowers and soils — the inevitable context for the survival of most of earth's people.

> Then He spoke many things to them in parables, saying: "Behold, a sower went out to sow.
> "And as he sowed, some seed fell by the wayside; and the birds came and devoured them.
> "Some fell on stony places, where they did not have much earth; and they immediately sprang up because they had no depth of earth.
> "But when the sun was up they were scorched, and because they had no root they withered away.
> "And some fell among thorns, and the thorns sprang up and choked them.
> "But others fell on good ground and yielded a crop: some a hundredfold, some sixty, some thirty.
> "He who has ears to hear, let him hear!"
>
> Matthew 13:3-9

It is at the end of this parable that the disciples question the use of parables and receive Jesus' answer, which we have already examined. And, as we will see, Jesus *Himself* explains His use of this particular parable in verses 18-23.

Agriculture is a favorite source on which Jesus based many of His stories. Luke records the same story in a context that is similar to Matthew's account, yet with several dissimilarities, including an emphasis that is clearly different. *"...The seed is the word of God,"* he quotes Jesus as saying (Luke 8:11).

48

Luke's context includes the family members coming *after*, not before, this incident. He also combines this parable with other unrelated parables, as well as several stories and miracles that took place in Jesus' ministry. Thus, Luke's account of this particular parable is clearly not related within a single discourse of Jesus; rather, it is remembered and placed in a Lucan context in accord with the evangelist's overall presentation.

Perhaps such contextual explanation bores you. Believe me, it is prerequisite to understanding the obvious first question regarding Jesus' chosen beginning explanation of the Kingdom in Matthew 13.

Luke's context is not about the Kingdom at all, but rather about the provision and care of Jesus' physical needs by a group of wealthy women drawing from their own substance. Luke is clearly following the immediate growth of Jesus' ministry and its impact on various elements of society. He even reveals all of this parable before the sending out of the seventy. On the other hand, Matthew's recording of Jesus' important "house divided" speech, which is the context of the Pharisees' hostility against Jesus and leads to His Kingdom discourse, is not even mentioned by Luke until many events *after* His parable of the sower.

Isn't it possible that Jesus used the story on two occasions with different applications? Many teachers believe this to be true. Regardless, you can be assured that only Matthew sees this particular parable as fundamental to a specifically arranged discourse of Jesus on the nature and principles of the Kingdom of God.

## 'The Casting of a Man'

Let us review carefully Jesus' discussion of the parable of the sower in Matthew.

> "Therefore hear the parable of the sower:
> "When anyone hears the word of the kingdom, and does
> not understand it, then the wicked one comes and snatches

away what was sown in his heart. This is he who received seed by the wayside.

"But he who received the seed on stony places, this is he who hears the word and immediately receives it with joy;

"yet he has no root in himself, but endures only for a while. For when tribulation or persecution arises because of the word, immediately he stumbles.

"Now he who received seed among the thorns is he who hears the word, and the cares of this world and the deceitfulness of riches choke the word, and he becomes unfruitful.

"But he who received seed on the good ground is he who hears the word and understands it, who indeed bears fruit and produces: some a hundredfold, some sixty, some thirty."

Matthew 13:18-23

This explanation makes it clear that this parable is definitely different from Luke's explanation of the other parable of the seeds and sower.

Let me be clear and thorough. There are many contemporary writers who say, based on comparison, that this is the same story and conclusion. The seed is "the Word of God" and the response concerns all the various types of soil that interact to produce success or failure. This is one common understanding. We write plays and skits to make this parable illustrative of Gospel witness.

I must admit this interpretation fits conveniently into our prevailing Christian emphasis. We do our job — sowing the Word, generally impersonally — and it's the stony soil or "rock" that makes the seed we sow ineffective. Certainly no blame can be placed on us!

Clearly Jesus "upsets the apple cart" in the Matthew discourse with His explanation of the second parable: *"The field is the world, the good seeds are the sons of the kingdom, but the tares are the sons of the wicked one"* (Matt. 13:38). Now, you can simply conclude, as do many current writers, that Jesus' use of metaphor in this parable is different than in His first parable. *But that presents a problem, for it would entail that Jesus changed metaphors in a single set discourse.*

Is the correct conclusion to this matter really that simple? G. Campbell Morgan writes, "The seed is *not* the Word — cast into the heart of a man. (That is in Luke's account: Luke 8:1-15.) *But it is the CASTING of a MAN into a certain age and generation.... It is a sowing, not of truth, but of man....*"[29]

Can this be? If so, it turns everything we knew about Kingdom purpose on its head! Is the Kingdom purpose to plant the Word, scattering the seed here and there so that it sporadically bears fruit, depending on soil or climatic conditions? Or does God plant *people*? Does He carefully scatter prepared sons and daughters of the Kingdom throughout the world in every age or era for the fulfillment of His purposes?

I don't know about you, but I am forever grateful to the Father that He didn't send a tract or write a book, however well graphically designed. *God sent His Son.* We call that incarnation "the Truth in flesh"; "the Message in the Man"; "the Christ Man"; or "the God Man."

Our ability to grasp the rest of this sermon of Jesus hangs very clearly on how we read this parable. Vincent, in his often-quoted *Word Studies of the New Testament*, writes:

> He which received seed (*ó spareís*). Lit., and much better, Rev., *He that was sown;* identifying the *seed* of the figure with the *man* signified.[30]

Kienecker and Rogers in *Linguistic Key to the Greek New Testament* agree:

> *ésparménon* perfect passive participle *speíro, oútos.* This refers to the person, not the seed (McNeile). *spareís* aorist passive participle *speíro.*[31]

Archibald Thomas Robertson sees the confusion but places it in context:

"This is he" (*houtos estin*). Matthew, like Mark, speaks of the people who hear the words as the seed itself. That creates some confusion in this condensed form of what Jesus actually said, but the real point is clear. *The seed sown in his heart* (*to esparmenon en tei kardiai autou*, perfect passive participle of *speiro*, to sow) and "the man sown by the wayside" (*ho para ten hodon spareis*, aorist passive participle, along the wayside) are identified. The seed in the heart is not of itself responsible, but the man who lets the devil snatch it away.[32]

It is the conclusion I argue for most, rather than a debate on the specifics. More radical than an argument of Greek verbs or word order is the statement of purpose, for here is a radically different concept of how the Kingdom of God strategizes its influence, disciples its people, and ultimately "rests its case."

*God plants the Son or Daughter of the Kingdom in the middle of an age that is against the King. There in that place, he or she will exert an incredible influence that will tell eternally for the Kingdom of God.*

When the world bumps into a true Kingdom representative, they run headlong into God. This is why being raised up for the Kingdom provides a purpose larger than that of either the Church or Israel. The Church becomes a sacrament of the Kingdom — the living type of the Kingdom of Heaven, or the Kingdom of God. *But the Kingdom is greater than the Church.* Every true decision, philosophy, and strategy of the Church should be based on this premise. When Christians embrace this foundational understanding, almost everything changes; very little indeed remains the same.

# 7 KINGDOM SEED – KINGDOM PEOPLE

A re you staggered a bit? If what we have discussed so far is true, the measure of our personal discipleship and our training of others has a relatively specific basis for evaluation: *What effect are we producing on the age we live in?* God has something for us to influence on our way to Heaven. He has raised us up for the purposes of His Kingdom.

## The Condition of the Seed

In Jesus' first parable of Matthew 13, He clearly makes *no* reference to the sower, only to the seed and its relationship to the soil. As we have seen, it is easy to conclude that the chief lessons of the parable are to be discovered in the soil. It is only in Christ's explanation that we learn this is not the case at all. *The emphasis is on the condition of the seed cast into the soil, not on whether the soil is an open highway, a rocky place, or thorny ground.*

> "Therefore hear the parable of the sower:
> "When anyone hears the word of the kingdom, and does not understand it, then the wicked one comes and snatches away what was sown in his heart. *This is he who received seed by the wayside.*"
>
> Matthew 13:18,19

Notice in verse 19 that Jesus says, "This is *he*...," *not* "This is *it*...." In each of the following explanations, it is the responsibility of *him who receives*. Ten times in the explanation there is the uncomfortable emphasis on *he*. Remember Morgan's words, *"It is the sowing, not of truth, but of men."* Or again, consider the words of Archibald Robertson: "The seed in the heart is not of itself responsible, but the man who lets the devil snatch it away." *The correct focus must again and again be reiterated: the eternal effect of a Kingdom person who influences his age for the Kingdom of God!*

## Misdirected Kingdom Purpose

Chè Ahn, an Asian-born leader in the contemporary American church, made the notable comment while preaching in our church: "We have to forget about *just* our churches and our agendas and concentrate on the Kingdom of God." We can thus see the value of our study in Matthew 13. Understanding Jesus' meaning here would forever save us from indulging in superfluous language, effort, and explanation. Let us not be well-meaning but deluded disciples!

The gigantic biblical example of misdirection regarding this principle was Israel. God's judgment on His people inevitably had an underlying reason. Israel's chore was to enlighten the Gentiles and to witness to the world. Their failed witness even more than other lifestyle issues brought God's ultimate judgment. They were to be God's light, not God's spoiled brats.

How then does God judge our ministries, our churches? By the size or quality of our buildings or by the number of bodies sitting in the pews? I think not.

## Examples of True Kingdom Purpose

In Bulgaria, where I often minister, the contemporary church is just coming out of years of persecution and thus lacks many of the accouterments of successful Western ministry. *However, they have fostered an understanding of influentially planting their people in society.*

54

For example, a young classical violinist named Bojadarva (meaning "Gift of God") plays artistically and professionally with a unique Christian commitment and discipline. Her concerts, often attended by conservatory teachers, demonstrate her influence. Then there is Stephen Vrachev, a young Christian man who has alone been given the privilege of playing the national organ in Sophia. Yet Stephen delights in leading his Sunday worship group with a humble keyboard instrument. Another Bulgarian Christian, often found at the keyboard of *his* church worship team, was recently named the Bulgarian composer of the year. Now, *that's* getting it right!

Several American Christian youth bands such as D. C. Talk, Delirious, and Jars of Clay are influencing their generation for God by crossing over into popular music while maintaining a consistent focus and godly lifestyle. *Remember, when a son or daughter of the Kingdom is planted in the midst of an era that is antagonistic to the King, that person will TELL for the Kingdom!*

I believe the Holy Spirit wants to get this message across to us so distinctly. Our job is ultimately not to focus on gathering people into our church building; it is much grander than that. Nor is it our task to simply get people saved and then familiarize them with church ritual until we wear them out. We have a responsibility to disciple people until we can confidently release them into this world, scattering them to bear influence on this age for the Kingdom of God.

## Our Mission Field — The World We Live In

And so it ultimately comes back to us. How well do we disciple and then release? We must never lay hands on every new convert and tie their lives to the ritual of church activity. The Church, although God's chosen vessel, is nonetheless a sacrament of the Kingdom of God, which is the entity that will supercede all else.

Too often we focus on the bright and most talented new converts. We not-so-subtly lay hands upon these new believers, ordaining them to full-time positions in the church organization. We even suggest that there is a "highest" call to strive for, allowing new converts to infer the message that stepping into the so-called "full-time" ministry is God's *first place* for the ordination of people; everything else is second place.

Now, I've been delighted to have been in such full-time service most of my life as evangelist, administrator, teacher, and pastor. But my ultimate test, like those to whom I minister, is larger than my assignment or my sixty-hour work week. It rests in the answer to this question: *What effect is my life producing for the Kingdom of God?*

I'm not trying to make you angry, but there is a point here that I feel compelled to stress. I speak from the standpoint of one who has many years in the ministry. I have taught at Bible schools and seminaries and have had more than the usual number of ministers and missionaries describe my life as having been influential, even life-directing. And I am telling you that if God calls you to be a preacher and it is His specific will, of course you must do it. *But if there is any way you can escape — run!*

It would be against the plan of God to bind the most successful business people, the finest administrators, or the most influential teachers to the institutional church. We must send them into the world. *They are sown into this age to revolutionize and change this era for the purposes of the Kingdom of God.* We cannot afford to let the world take over every arena of life, such as the media, publishing, television, movies, popular music, and the internet.

A church where I frequently minister has a sign on the exit road from their facility to the public road. "You are about to enter the mission field." *That's it!*

Perhaps we should admit that many evangelical Christians *love souls but dislike people.* It is certainly true that our evangelism almost always has a built-in distance factor. We like television, literature, and stadium crusades. Yet statistics consistently show that more than eighty percent of all people who find Christ come to Him through the contact of a family member, business associate, friend, or acquaintance. Less than twenty percent are directly attributed to the built-in "distance factor" evangelism of the Church, such as literature, mass crusades, or media evangelism.

"But aren't we supposed to hate the world?" you may ask. "Are we not to come out of the world and touch it not?"

*Clearly, not at all.* The Scripture differentiates between the world of people, whom God loves and for whom Christ died; the world of creation, which originated in the heart of the Triune God and is a constant voice of His power in every language; and a subtly hostile world of anti-God materialism and destructive ideas.

The believer must accept his role of stewardship by manifesting love and compassion in the first and second worlds. Only the third definition provides an arena of warfare, separation, and intense loathing to the Christian. That "third world," which is under the control of Satan, enslaves and destroys. The Christian is right to hate it!

But, oh, how often the institutional church mixes its metaphors and confuses people! We not only withdraw from the wrong "world" — we welcome the wrong influence. Even theology becomes success-oriented, and pyramid-scheme groups rush to the church to find their suckers. If all the hidden, unsold soap products buried in Christian basements would suddenly explode, the earth would experience an instant car wash! *Someone got the message wrong!*

The apostle Paul must have felt the same exasperation on this subject that I often do, as indicated in what he wrote in First Corinthians 5:

> **I wrote to you in my epistle not to keep company with sexually immoral people.**

Yet I certainly did not mean with the sexually immoral people of this world, or with the covetous, or extortioners, or idolaters, *since then you would need to go out of the world.*

1 Corinthians 5:9,10

Oh, really, Paul. What then did you mean?

But now I have written to you not to keep company with anyone named a brother, who is sexually immoral, or covetous, or an idolater, or a reviler, or a drunkard, or an extortioner — not even to eat with such a person.

1 Corinthians 5:11

Well, now, that puts the shoe on a different foot. But Paul isn't finished.

For what have I to do with judging those also who are outside? Do you not judge those who are inside?

1 Corinthians 5:12

I know so many Christians who would be totally free if they only understood these words and the Christian philosophy they represent. These words fit clearly in the context of a multitude of other scriptures and convey the message that *acceptance is not approval.*

The call of God on those of us who are Christians is marvelously exciting. We are ambassadors of Christ, pleading with the world to be reconciled to God since *He* has been reconciled to *them* through the blood of His Son and no longer counts their trespasses against them (2 Cor. 5:18-21).

# 8 FRUIT IN OUR AGE

P arables were stories that Jesus took from the commonplace experience of the people. The first and foundational parable in Jesus' important teaching on the Kingdom of God was no exception. The experience of sowing seed was directly related to everyday life.

In rural Israel, there were many places where only stony soil could be found; yet the ground nevertheless had to be sown. There were also beaten-down paths created by people walking through otherwise fruitful fields. And, of course, there were the ever-present birds that kept a lookout for poorly sown seed or seed that had fallen on hard ground.

Besides all these obstacles to harvest, the sower had to deal with the excruciatingly hot Palestinian summer. Seed that had not gained quick access to moistened soil would quickly dry out. Yet in spite of all the enemies of harvest, the Galilean hills of Jesus' day grew many harvests and supported a burgeoning population.[33]

## 'He Who Is Sown'
## For God's Kingdom

As we have seen, however, in Jesus' explanation of the Matthew 13 parable, *He casts a responsibility on the man who is symbolized by the seed.* Although some translations continue to render, *"This is he who received seed...,"* the more accurate translation is *"This is he who was sown...."*

The seed and the man are one. As Vincent explains, "He that was sown; identifying the seed of the figure with the man signified."[34] Let us not belabor this point and thus encourage argument among those of differing views. Instead, let us agree that if we accept this explanation, the following four illustrations of results speak directly to our thesis. Each parable speaks of the way the Church, acting as a sacrament of the Kingdom, *prepares and releases seed* to be sown into the present age.

As we will clearly see in the development of this discourse, there is one good Sower, Jesus Christ Himself; one kind of seed, the men and women of the Kingdom of God; and one kind of soil, the current age. But to our astonishment, there are four totally different results to the sowing, depending on the nature of response that Kingdom folk have when confronted with their present-day Kingdom challenges.

Although the characteristic expression of eras changes, the overall conflict remains the same. I am not responsible for my father's generation. Dramatically saved from a life of alcoholism and gangs, Dad became a unique seed of God, sown by the divine Sower into a unique generation of World Wars, a serious national Depression, and convulsing religious movements. The effect of my father's life for the Kingdom of God was marked, and the fruit remains.

Dad cannot serve the age I live in any more than I can reach back to alter the direction of the age *he* lived in. Yet we have been sown in the same way and for the same ultimate purpose — to influence our own era with the eternal principles of the Kingdom of God.

(I love you, Dad. I believe somehow you pray for me in my unique battles for the Kingdom.)

In G. Campbell Morgan's excellent commentary on Matthew, he relates the following:

> It is not a question of the creation of the Church by the gathering of individual men to Himself, but rather of the establishment of the Kingdom. Here, then, is the method of His work during this age — the sowing of the sons of the Kingdom. Some of them are productive. Some of them bring forth fruit, fruit that is toward the Kingdom. They influence the age, creating in it the recognition of, and approximation to the government of God. Others produce no such fruit. They are men who come into contact with the thought of the Kingdom and the ideals of the Kingdom, but who never produce the fruit of the Kingdom.[35]

No summary I might make could be more clear. The question must always center around fruit for God's Kingdom — godly influence produced by Kingdom men and women in a godless age.

## Have We Counted the Cost?

Surely now the four separate examples of our Master speak conviction to our understanding of our leadership role in this age.

"How so?" you ask. "Can it really be both ways?"

Let me illustrate from more than thirty years as a senior pastor of a growing church. Performing weddings can become an overwhelming chore and responsibility, as well as a great privilege. I have always asked for a minimum of four premarital sessions with the engaged couple, which include both personality inventories and vulnerable discussion.

The first of these sessions is a "get-acquainted session." In this preliminary session, I inquire through many questions about the couple's personal relationship, as well as about their understanding of marriage. But I want them to leave both honest *and* exposed. So before they leave, I very truthfully line up current statistics and common horror stories of marital failure.

The couple generally leaves this session shaking their heads and working through growing doubt — which is exactly how it should be. *No one should get married until they have to!*

That's why I encourage couples to move toward marriage only when they sense a certain inevitability in following the will and purpose of God for their lives. On more than one occasion, this counsel has resulted in a frustrated mother calling me to say, "What are you doing? We already have the caterer and have printed the napkins!"

In spite of all this realism, I rarely succeed in changing anyone's mind. Soon I am standing before this couple in a room filled with friends and family. The groom looks *so* uncomfortable in his tuxedo as he constantly fiddles with the tight collar. The bride, however, looks radiant, as though she had taken nineteen years to prepare for this one moment!

When I ask the groom to repeat the extremely serious and life-threatening vows of marriage, his outward demeanor often seems to be saying, "I will. I do. Let's get this over with!" I have always threatened to one day grab such a nervous bridegroom by the collar and say, "Hey! Do you know what you just said?"

*Of course, the groom does NOT know what he just said.* But life experience will soon teach him the reality of every word!

So it is when we receive Jesus as our Savior and confess with our mouth His Lordship and sovereignty over our lives. Did we understand all our decision would mean in the years that followed? Or were we so infatuated with the forgiveness of sins and the promise of eternal life that we never really counted the cost?

The second illustration Jesus uses in the first parable is a man who, when he hears the Word, "receives it with joy" (Matt. 13:20). However, because this person is not yet rooted, he easily stumbles when confronted with tribulation.

It is at this point that we must cry out, "That's it! Here is the explanation of so much that we face on a daily basis in our work for the Kingdom of God."

Truly the difference between a believer who doesn't count the cost — who stops growing after being justified by faith through Calvary — and a believer who continually lives out the purposes of God's Kingdom is like night and day!

## Sown To Reveal Divine Purpose

Our Heavenly Father is a very good Steward and a wonderful Farmer. When He desired to impact the age of man, He did not send a tract. Instead, He sent His Son, born of flesh and made like man in every way. The Father incarnated the hidden truth of eternal purpose in the Person and personality of the Son, Jesus Christ. Then the Son, by His faithful and sacrificial obedience, revealed the purpose of the Father to mankind.

In just the same way, Jesus, as the Steward of the Father's world, sows into every age sons and daughters of the Kingdom (John 20:21). They are meant, as Jesus was, to influence and alter the direction of the current age through their godly lives, their God-given gifts, and their compassionate concern. They are meant to be world-changers, influencing every arena of life in the era of their generation.

# 9 KINGDOM PERCENTAGES

B y now, certain phrases should be rolling around in your mind and heart. For instance, remember the words of George Ladd, who said, "For Jesus, the kingdom of God was *the dynamic rule of God* which had invaded history in His own Person...." You may also remember that he gives a statement of purpose, which is in truth the focus of his discussion on the purpose of the Kingdom: *"...to bring men in the present age the blessings of the messianic age...."* What higher or more relevant call could come to any man or woman?

Then there were the words of Alexander Maclaren, who stated that the purpose of Jesus' teaching in Matthew 13 is "to reveal rather the conditions of the growth of the Kingdom in human society." Amazing. Such a concept certainly changes the barometer!

## Things Are Not Always as They Seem

Things indeed are not always as they seem. Consider the current warnings on automobile mirrors that say, *"Objects may be closer than they appear."* Yipes! Perhaps God's timetable, as well as His ultimate purpose, has eluded us.

I once heard about a white-haired senior woman who, after shopping, came out to discover four young white males about to drive off with her car. She dropped her shopping bags, pulled a handgun from her purse, and shouted, *"I have a handgun, and I know how to use it! Get out of my car, you scumbags!"*

Terrified, the four young men leapt simultaneously out of the car and fled the parking lot. Badly shaken by her experience, the older lady then loaded her groceries into the car and prepared to drive away. She was so shaken, however, that she could not get the key into the ignition. She tried and tried, but to no avail. Finally, she discovered the problem — she spotted her *own* car, parked four spaces away!

After quickly transferring her groceries to her car, the woman promptly drove to the police station. The policeman to whom she told the story practically collapsed with laughter as he directed the lady's attention to the end of the counter. There stood four very pale young men, in the process of reporting a car-jacking by "an older lady, about five feet tall, with white curly hair, carrying a very large handgun"!

What is the lesson to be learned? *Things do not always appear as they actually are.*

No wonder Jesus warned, *"Do not judge according to appearance, but judge with righteous judgment"* (John 7:24). We need to know God's actual program for the church of Jesus Christ in this era. Then we must be prepared to willfully and intelligently cooperate with that purpose.

## Integrating Spiritual Purpose With Secular Life

Jesus said in Matthew 13:19, *"When anyone hears the word of the kingdom, and does not understand it, then the wicked one comes and snatches away what was sown in his heart. This is he who received seed* [literally, he who was sown] *by the wayside."* Now, remember — it is "the word of the Kingdom" at stake here, *not* salvation. The question asked in this entire teaching is *the success of production* — the influence waged upon the era for the Kingdom of God.

You must notice in Jesus' first example that no overt emphasis is given to the environs — in this case, the wayside. The blame is not placed on the wayside where the seed was sown. What is missing is *the man*. He "does not understand it" — this word of the Kingdom.

The Greek word here for "understand" is *suniemi*, which primarily means *to set* or *to bring together*. Metaphorically, we would say that the man in this parable is supposed *to perceive* or *to unite* the truth to his life.

Another definition is *the perception of what is perceived*. Thus, the word often refers, in a moral and spiritual sense, to a lack of wisdom. We might say that the man in this first example did not unite (*sun*) or integrate his spiritual purpose with his secular life. No eternal issue resulted from his planting, no divine influence to his age. In the end, he supplied nothing that made God's Kingdom nearer or more real to the natural eye.

We recognize this case, if not this person. He may succeed well in the institutional belief structure and setting. However, he has no clearly established relationships outside that institutional structure because he has never synthesized and united his knowledge of Kingdom responsibility with his career or secular placement. Even the concept of his divine placement in the world has been snatched away.

## The Need To Prepare the Seed

Client two hears the word of the Kingdom and *"...immediately receives it with joy"* (v. 20). Obviously, this man goes further than the first. In this second example, the man not only clearly hears the word of the Kingdom, but he becomes familiar with its truth and *specifically consents to its claim*. He knows himself to be sown, and he understands the Father's purpose, rejoicing in the fact that he has been strategically placed to influence his age and his generation for the Kingdom of God.

But there is a hitch: *"Yet he has no root in himself, but endures only for a while. For when tribulation or persecution arises because of the word, immediately he stumbles"* (Matt. 13:21). This believer has never allowed the word to firmly take root. He certainly cannot influence his age for the Kingdom of God. Instead, he becomes a nonproductive seed in the soil.

But let us be clear. A primary sowing *had* occurred previously — the mysterious divine impartation by which all seeds are given full equality to produce a harvest.

Sons and daughters of the Kingdom are right where they are supposed to be — in the world, in this age. People are not second-class Christians because they work in the business world, in the media, or in hospitals. They are no less than the minister because they teach in public schools, drive cabs, or operate an industrial assembly line. They were sown there. But how do they become prepared to stand for the Kingdom in their appointed place?

The local church where Christians meet for fellowship, training, and communion is not the Kingdom, although clearly it is a sacrament of the Kingdom. Given that fact, doesn't the institutional church and its leaders have a responsibility *not simply* to evangelize, reconciling men and women to Jesus Christ, but *to teach them their purpose in the Kingdom and help them to stand*?

Jesus clearly prepared His disciples. He warned them that in the world, they would have tribulation. He modeled before them the godly response to hostility, misunderstanding, and outright attack. He took them to various scriptures to help them understand the nature of believing within an angry and godless society.

As a result of the Master's wise preparation, the disciples generally stood fast. Some may have done it fearfully; others learned through failure. Ultimately, however, all but one stood firm.[36]

Tribulation is an interesting word in the original language. The Greek word translated is *thlipsis* and primarily means *pressure*. The English word "tribulation" comes even more clearly from the Latin word *tribulo*, a word most commonly associated with crushing grapes to produce wine.

If our second Kingdom candidate — one who begins with a joyous acceptance of the Kingdom word — fails to influence his age because he *stumbles* in its application within the context of persecution, whose fault is it? His own, ultimately and finally. But is anyone else at fault? Was this person prepared for the conflict?

Perhaps the evangelistic mindset of the Church needs to be turned around. Perhaps getting people "saved" is not enough. We must also disciple and release people into this age, into this world. The blame really does often come back to us.

As a pastor for the better part of a half century, I have been amazed at all the true Christians I've seen who were released into this world and stood tall and fast against the winds of trouble. That may in fact be the most eloquent witness a Kingdom son or daughter will ever provide.

When I think of the fruit that has remained in our congregation, I realize that it has often been produced by those who stood unbending in the winds of adversity and, in the process, won incredibly open opportunities to bring Kingdom truth into their age and era. In one such case, a wife battled cancer in one of those inexplicable struggles. She seemed to be the aggressive partner in terms of faith, and many people questioned what would happen to Bill if Joanne was not healed.

Would you like to know the truth of what did happen? Brothers in the Lord walked with Bill in discipleship and, through encouragement, he became stronger and stronger instead of becoming discouraged or faithless. In the process, Bill grew more solid and strongly rooted. As never before, he began to clearly influence those around him for the Gospel of Jesus Christ and the principles of God's Kingdom.

The most challenging circumstances we face are often the most public and social issues of our lives. But we need not stumble. In truth, there will never be more opportune times in which we are called to stand.

## The *Influencer* Who Becomes the *Influenced*

The third of Jesus' four examples of Kingdom seed — men and women sown by God's Spirit into the world to influence their age for the King — is described as *"...he who received seed among the thorns..."* (v. 22). Here Jesus is referring to the person *"...who hears the word, and the cares of this world and the deceitfulness of riches choke the word, and he becomes unfruitful."*

It appears that this case is very unlike the others. This person embraces his divine placement. He is in fact "worldly" in the sense of knowing where he's meant to be for the purposes of the God's Kingdom. However, the message of the Kingdom is choked out because of the influence of riches and the cares of life. Complacency and compromise produce the silence required to focus on accumulating earthly riches.

*Again, note God's clearly unmet expectation regarding this person* in Jesus' closing word: *"...and he becomes unfruitful."* Nothing in this parable indicates that the issue we are dealing with here is whether or not these Kingdom candidates are saved.

This third man, represented by the "thorny ground," has within him the life-giving principle that can eternally influence his age for the Kingdom of God. But he is simply too overwhelmed with the *things* of this age — its methods, its maxims, its cares, and its pleasures. Like growing and thickening thorns, the cares of this life and the deceitfulness of riches have choked out the vital principle of why this man is here on this earth and what he is called to do. He is prevented from having any effect *on* the age in which he lives because he has allowed himself to be overcome *by* it. He has become the *influenced*, not the *influencer*.

## Good Ground
## Equals Productive Ground

In this parable of Kingdom seed, Jesus finally describes the man who by his response becomes "good ground." This man clearly hears the word of the Kingdom and *understands* it (v. 23). Note carefully that his success comes from his ability to integrate the Word with his divine purpose. This man is not always a hundredfold successful; sometimes he produces only a thirtyfold or a sixtyfold result. *Nevertheless, he is always producing.* He obeys the Word and produces fruit in his age — the true requirement and test for all Kingdom sons and daughters.

We have noted earlier that the overwhelming percentage of Christians were won to the Lord by fathers, mothers, business associates, friends, and lovers — ordinary people who influenced their era by growing and producing wherever they were planted. Also, it is said that three out of ten people who are unreached from a Christian viewpoint are living within reach of a Kingdom person.

I know many such Kingdom people. For instance, one pastor I know makes a point of taking another pastor to lunch each week. He simply goes through the phone book, using no other criteria than a desire to meet and pray with some other Christian leader. Another Christian I know takes some government official to lunch every Wednesday. He has no agenda other than a clear desire to influence for God the "influencers" of his age.

As we ourselves seek to affect this present-day age for the Kingdom of God, let us not be overcome with protocol or overwhelmed by religious agenda. No matter what purpose we are striving to accomplish, it will only be fulfilled as we are empowered by the Spirit of God.

Nevertheless, let us recognize that we are all influencers. Our age should bear the mark that we were here. We may assume that our power is limited and our influence is insignificant, but there are youth teams to be coached, senior centers to be visited, the handicapped to be helped, officials to be appreciated, and projects to be completed. *Let the word of the Kingdom in us produce a desire to serve its agenda.*

How better to proclaim this timeless message than from a passage in Isaiah, read by Jesus Himself in His first public synagogue appearance:

> "The Spirit of the Lord is upon Me, because He has anointed Me to preach the gospel to the poor; He has sent Me to heal the brokenhearted, to proclaim liberty to the captives and recovery of sight to the blind, to set at liberty those who are oppressed;
> "To proclaim the acceptable year of the Lord."
>
> Luke 4:18,19[37]

What better description of the effect we are to have on the age we live in! God has given us the divine mandate. Now it is up to us to produce fruit for the Kingdom in the soil where we have been sown according to His eternal purposes.

# 10 SOWING IS RELEASING

For many years I have been associated on an adjunct basis with two seminaries — graduate institutions focused on ministerial and leadership preparation for the church. Many denominations require a degree from such institutions in order to become ordained in their churches. Yet other people change the name of these seminaries to *cemeteries*, and they warn hungry students that the critical nature of graduate study will consume their lives and limit their "power." In reality, however, no institution can either give away ministry or be the ultimate death of true vision!

But, after all, the etymology of the word "seminary," an English word, is connected (rather embarrassingly) to the word "semen." A seminary, then, is meant to be connected to that which is seminal, or that which has to do with *seed*. One stuffy, classical dictionary states that someone who attends a seminary is "a person occupied in sowing seed."[38] Now there's a concept I can get into!

Regardless of a person's title, degrees, or position, he only gets into this "sower's club" if he knows what to do with seed in a productive, eternal, and continuing type of way. Otherwise, he is merely a keeper of keys, a collector of trivia, or a braggart of degrees.

## The True Meaning of Seed-Sowing

*A seed-sower is a biblical person*, someone who knows to guard seed and who understands the soil, the age, the era. He is also someone who guards the future of planting and who believes in the future of harvest. This kind of person is a hot item, a longed-for product in a greatly needed career!

The seed we work with, as Jesus clearly taught, is not simply "the word of the Kingdom," as preeminently important as that is. It also includes the sowing of men and women into a certain age or generation. We can't ever forget that the Gospel is ultimately incarnate. First and foremost is the living incarnation of the Word in Jesus Christ, our Lord and Savior. However, the Word is also to be continuously incarnated in the released lives of Kingdom men and women into the world.

*How tragic that the institutional church builds bigger barns to store this Kingdom seed while the enemy silently takes over the winds of the harvest:* the media, the publishing field, movies, cultural styles, and education. Remember, "broadcast" is originally a word bound up with sowing seed. God intends to profoundly affect this current age through the presence, lives, and influence of those who have not only heard the Word, but who have also received it and obeyed it.

Carlos Annacondia, the great Argentine evangelist often referred to as the Billy Graham of South America, attended a Sunday morning church service in Buenos Aires where I was speaking. When we were introduced, he said, "The Lord spoke to me this morning and said, 'When you build larger and more beautiful churches to house Christians, you glorify man. But when you release Christians into the world to be fruitful, you glorify God.'"

A prolific and controversial writer, Robert Farrar Capon, writes this statement about the Kingdom of God:

It means that it is not about *someplace else called heaven, nor about somebody at a distance called God.* Rather it is about *this place here* in all its "this-ness" and "place-ness," and about the intimate and immediate Holy One Who, at no distance from us at all, moves mysteriously to make creation *true* both to itself and to Him. That, I take it, is the force of phrases like "the city of God" and "the Kingdom of God." They say to me that the Bible is concerned with the perfecting of what God made, not with the trashing of it — with the resurrection of its native harmonies and orders, not with the replacement of them by something else.[39]

So the Church, as the sacrament and living type of the Kingdom of God, accepts as its basic methodology the word of the here and now: To sow sons and daughters of the Kingdom who are prepared to bring forth fruit for the Kingdom. These individuals are meant to not only influence the age they live in, but also to produce through their own lives both the recognition of and an approximation to the government of God.

## On With the Game!

In a second major parable in Matthew 13, Jesus clearly says, *"The field is the world, the good seeds are the sons of the kingdom, but the tares are the sons of the wicked one"* (Matt. 13:38). The field is the world, indeed! Within the world of human society, the Lord Jesus has scattered His own seed. *We* are the seed of Jesus.

Perhaps this is why the anger of Jesus burned particularly bright against religious leaders:

> **"Woe to you, scribes and Pharisees, hypocrites! For you pay tithe of mint and anise and cummin, and have neglected the weightier matters of the law:** *justice and mercy and faith....*"
>
> Matthew 23:23

The candidates in the first parable who had their placement snatched away, who stumbled in the midst of tribulation, or who became choked by cares and riches, were all judged by one standard —

75

no fruitfulness, no influence. Perhaps, as I believe, *they were never directed toward their purpose.*

Perhaps the church should develop ordination services for nurses, cab drivers, businessmen and women, physicians, and teachers. These sons and daughters of the Kingdom are put right where God wants them — in the world.

Wherever we are, as children of God and as sons or daughters of the Kingdom, we have been put there by the Lord Jesus. It is so important to understand that He has sown us and placed us where we are. We are to gather with the rest of our local church for worship, instruction, and fellowship. But then it is time to go out and become an influence for God's Kingdom where we have been placed.

In a sense, the church pews or chairs should face backwards. Imagine if the congregation came roaring out of the church like a football team from their locker room! Enough pep talks — let's get on with the game!

## Examples of Strategic Placement

While I am writing this book, the United States, in cooperation with many other nations, is engaged in a worldwide conflict to deal with terrorists in every place they are found. The outcome of so vast a project is always in question, although the need is more apparent with every day that passes.

It is a critical moment of history, perhaps fraught with eschatological significance. The horrors of September 11, 2001, when the World Trade Towers were reduced to rubble by American passenger planes commandeered and turned into deadly missiles, have forever changed our lives and our sense of security as a nation. Stories are emerging almost daily of Christians who were strategically placed during this tragedy.

When I was a young man, fresh from graduate school and preparing to "change the world," I was recruited to serve at a Christian liberal arts college as dean of men and the director of student life. Both the dean of students and the president of the college were active in recruiting me and subsequently became giants on the "influence board" of my life. The president was a man of prayer with an eminent commitment to the small-group principle. Time spent in Robert's office always had a wonderful impact.

Along with his wife, Robert had taught and administered in as many Bible schools and colleges as any man I ever met. Only God knows how many young people he blessed and encouraged as they prepared for full-time Christian service as ministers, missionaries, musicians, and teachers. What a phenomenal influence!

Robert also had a wonderful family. I often wished I could have overheard the conversations that transpired during his time with his loved ones. I do not wish to be presumptuous of his family life, but I believe he must have prayed at some time over his children. I also believe that in some way, Robert conveyed this message to them:

*"Children, if God calls you to be a minister or a missionary, I want you to know that your mother and I will pray for you and support you in every way possible. But if that is not how God leads you, if He places you outside the institution of the church to influence this age in some other way, then know also that we will pray for you and support you in the same manner."*

I know one son in that family whose college and graduate degrees directed him to serve the Kingdom of God through the influence of governmental involvement. Ultimately he became Attorney General of his home state Missouri; later he served for two terms as the Governor of Missouri. Building on his favor with God and man, this man was elected as a United States Senator from Missouri. Following that tenure, he was named to the highest law official position in this country and became the Attorney General of the United States.

The man's name is John Ashcroft. This strategic planting of Kingdom seed was made long before we knew such names as Al Qaeda and Bin Laden or experienced such a horrible loss of life on American soil. God's directive of this Kingdom seed was planned and purposeful, and many in the United States are grateful for John's integrity, his straightforward principles, and his courage.

G. Campbell Morgan wrote, "Wherever sorrow is assuaged, wherever wounds are healed, wherever love becomes the law of life, wherever men are loosed from the power of sin, *there* the Kingdom of God has come. And such a harvest is the result of the living seeds flung from the hands of the living Sower upon the soil...."[40] What a statement! What a projection of purpose! I believe Morgan's quote provides the clear direction of Paul's often-misused statement in Romans 8:

> For I consider that the sufferings of this present time are not worthy to be compared with the glory which shall be revealed in us.
> For the earnest expectation of the creation eagerly waits for the revealing of the sons of God.
> For the creation was subjected to futility, not willingly, but because of Him who subjected it in hope;
> because the creation itself also will be delivered from the bondage of corruption into the glorious liberty of the children of God.
>
> Romans 8:18-21

Now, I've been in the church long enough to have heard every kind of misapplied doctrine and experience from that text. Many teachings of the so-called "manifest sons of God" have laid forth a second or third work of grace that would somehow make Christians stand out. I could never quite understand what that extra work of grace was supposed to look like. Would Christians suddenly turn purple or have flashing rainbow colors over their heads? I think not. In fact, I must say with G. Campbell Morgan that *the sons and daughters of the Kingdom of God ARE manifest, and this age is a thousand times better than it would be without them.*

When the horrendous AIDS crisis began to sweep this nation and the world, many evangelicals could only point their fingers and make pronouncements of judgment. This was easy to do, since most of the early AIDS victims, particularly in the United States, were from a lifestyle deemed biblically and socially unacceptable.

However, many sons and daughters of God's Kingdom quietly came to understand their placement. A successful hotel manager in San Jose began acting as a chaplain to AIDS patients, ultimately organizing needed services and a band of available people to help. In Southern California, a young married "YWAM-er" (i.e., Youth With a Mission staff member) cleaned toilets for many months to win the respect of suspicious and even belligerent hospice administrators. They finally said to him, "If what you've done is the type of Christianity you represent, we free you to pray with as many patients as you wish."

## The Kingdom Requirement To Change

As we learn about examples of Kingdom influence such as these, we cannot fail to understand Jesus' words: *"But if I cast out demons with the finger of God, surely the kingdom of God has come upon you"* (Luke 11:20).

Indeed, "plant the son of the Kingdom in the midst of an age that is against the King, and he will exert an influence that will tell for the Kingdom."[41] And what is the purpose? It is *"...to bring men in the present age the blessings of the messianic age...."*[42]

Here then is the commission, the purpose, and the glorious privilege of the sons and daughters of God's Kingdom — not simply to enshrine Jesus Christ, but to *follow* Him. However, to follow Jesus means *to maintain a willingness to change.*

Christ shows us how to transform things "as they are" into things "as they ought to be." It's a new direction. We cannot occupy ourselves with the methodology of the newest religious fads or success stories.

God, change us. Make us radical! May we be changed, enlarged, redirected, and freshly anointed with Your power. Please, Lord, deliver us from mediocrity, repeated slogans, and self-satisfied analysis!

# 11

# DARN THE DARNELL

We begin now a look at only the second of seven parables in Matthew 13. There can be no question that this one is the "hinge" parable. Although spoken to the multitudes and recorded in verses 24-30, its interpretation, requested by the disciples, comes only after the multitude has been sent away and Jesus and His disciples have reentered the house. If we agree that this is a set discourse on the subject of the Kingdom of God, the placement of the parable is very strategic.

We have seen that Matthew 13 comes as a storm of criticism, even hatred, has gathered around Jesus, seemingly related directly to the sending out of the twelve disciples. (It would be good to review Jesus' commissioning of the twelve by reading the entire tenth chapter of Matthew.)

The second parable, often referred to as "the parable of the wheat and the tares," seems uniquely filled with pathos when one remembers the warfare and confusion that always accompanies true Kingdom of God strategy. Although no mystical dualism exists in this story or its explanation, there *is* obvious conflict — conflict that God finally resolves only at the end of the age.

Interestingly, both this parable and the final parable are found *only* in the book of Matthew. And both of these unique teachings include horrendous details of the final judgment that carry a purposeful emphasis, coming as they do from the mouth of the compassionate and sacrificial Savior, Jesus Christ. *How true it is that mercy and justice meet in this Man of all ages!*

It has been said that Jesus talks more about the everlasting consequences of man's actions than any other New Testament source. That fact should both strengthen and convict us. Herein indeed lies the balance.

## Two Sowings —
## The Wheat and the Tares

In the telling of this second parable, Jesus uses vivid word pictures to paint four easily understandable pictures depicting a responsible owner; an unexpected, malicious trespass; an ultimate quandary; and a surprising decision. Since our purpose will be better served by studying Jesus' subsequent explanation of the parable, our discussion of these four pictures will be limited. But again, we must keep in mind that the multitude received only this parable — and it was enough, based on Jesus' explanation of His *first* parable, to produce understanding and action.

First, Jesus establishes the presence of a responsible owner in the parable when He says, *"...The kingdom of heaven is like a man who sowed GOOD seed in his field"* (Matt. 13:24). The Greek word for the owner is *oikodespotes*, meaning *the lord of the house*. The field is the property of the man who sows the good seed. The proprietor is at work in his own field, sowing good seed with a desire to gather a definite harvest. Again, Jesus says that *the Kingdom of Heaven is like* this man and his venture. There is nothing so far that arrests one's attention.

However, we discover that two sowings take place as Jesus continues: *"But while men slept, his enemy came and sowed tares among the wheat and went his way"* (v. 25). Here is an unexpected and malicious trespass. It is a night picture. Sleeping does not imply that these were neglectful servants, although during planting and harvest time, both owners and servants often slept in their boundaried fields.

The owner clearly blames an "enemy," or literally "a man who is an enemy" for the offense. What this stealthy enemy sowed was *zizania* — weeds that, according to scholars, almost certainly contained the bearded *darnel*, also called *bastard wheat* by the Jews. The Hebrew word in fact seems connected to the word *zanah*, which has to do with fornication.

Darnel is mentioned eight times in Matthew 13. In its early stages, this weed is indistinguishable from the wheat and, in the end, must be laboriously separated. Otherwise, the consequences are very serious, for the grain of the "bearded darnel" is slightly poisonous and can cause dizziness and sickness. Even a small amount is bitter and unpleasant to taste.

Therefore, this second parable is referring to a spiteful, destructive, evil-minded, resentful, and malevolent sowing. To this day in some Eastern lands, the threat "I will sow bad seed in your field" is still made by a man to his enemy. Codified Roman law mentions and forbids this crime, laying down the punishment for an offender.

## 'Let Them Grow Together Until the Harvest'

At all young stages of growth, the darnel looks exactly like the wheat. Only at a significant stage of maturity can people distinguish the two. This leads to the ultimate quandary in Jesus' parable:

> "But when the grain had sprouted and produced a crop, then the tares also appeared.
> "So the servants of the owner came and said to him, 'Sir, did you not sow good seed in your field? How then does it have tares?'

"He said to them, 'An enemy has done this.' The servants said to him, 'Do you want us then to go and gather them up?'

Matthew 13:26-28

"Pull up the weeds." That seems to be an obvious conclusion, but the owner's quandary produces what is perhaps a surprising decision to the servants.

"But he said, 'No, lest while you gather up the tares you also uproot the wheat with them.
'Let both grow together until the harvest, and at the time of harvest I will say to the reapers, "First gather together the tares and bind them in bundles to burn them, but gather the wheat into my barn."'"

Matthew 13:29,30

To pull up the weed before it is fully grown does, without question, offer the potential of seriously damaging the true wheat plants that are growing alongside. In fact, some accounts say that the separation is only accurately made by spreading out the grain on a large tray after harvest. Workers are then able to easily pick out the darnel from the true wheat, for although the darnel seed is similar in shape and size to wheat, it is slate gray in color.[43]

Through this parable, the multitude was clearly left with a recognition that the Kingdom of God would suffer continuing violence from a real and hostile enemy. They also learned that the real enemy would seek to destroy the good seed before it could produce any fruit at all. This much was clear and vivid to the crowd of people who had come to hear Jesus teach. The Master would then teach them about the mustard seed and the leaven before sending them away. They had a lot to think about indeed concerning God's Kingdom purposes!

# 12 UNDERSTANDING THE PURPOSE OF THE KINGDOM

**B**efore we turn to the disciples' question concerning the wheat and tares, let us review Jesus' strategic question following His discourse concerning the Kingdom of God. He asked the disciples, *"...Have you understood all these things?"* (v. 51). Then He followed their response of *"Yes, Lord"* with that startling possibility: *"...Therefore every scribe instructed concerning the kingdom of heaven is like a householder who brings out of his treasure things new and old"* (v. 52).

## Interpreters of Divine Purpose

These teachings on the Kingdom are a syllabus, a curriculum so wide that they offer to a true student amazing potential that is both *practical* and *immediate.* The disciples were to take hold of an "old" idea and fulfill it, *for it would be those understanding the Kingdom of God who would become interpreters of the purposes of God.* Such men and women would become the *new* scribes, interpreters of the Kingdom through whom their age could know the issues concerning God's government.

There can be no doubt. Underlined here in the Master's teaching is the concept of *understanding.* Let me say it this way: *If*

85

*we have a wrong concept of the value and purpose of the Kingdom, our enthusiasm and devotion may be strong, but the influence of our service and its arena of action will be interfered with and therefore hindered.*

How much I see that in this era! So much misdirected activity takes place as a result of incorrect understanding. If service is to be truly effective and life-changing, it must be intelligently based on integration of Kingdom purpose with one's lifestyle and spiritual activity. This is why God gathers together a people in every age to become the revelation of His grace and love.

## The Ministry of the Kingdom 'Scribe'

The word "scribe," although used before the time of Ezra primarily to refer to *an expert in military logistics,* was clearly used after Ezra to represent *a student and teacher of God's Law.* However, by Jesus' day, scribes were obstinate individuals who clung tightly to tradition and ultimately stood bitterly opposed to Him.

Scribes were actually supposed to stand among the people, expounding the meaning of the Law to them by every means possible, including comment, exposition, and application. But by Jesus' day, they were giving just as much effort to interpreting oral tradition; meanwhile, their interpretation of the letter of the Law continued with an almost painful precision.

You may remember that King Herod's scribes were able to pinpoint Bethlehem with *absolute accuracy* as the birthplace of the coming Messiah (Matt. 2:4-6); yet they remained unmoved by the truth and unchanged by its fulfillment. G. Campbell Morgan writes concerning the scribes, "Their tradition had become a fence around the law in another sense than that intended, for, being a misinterpretation of the law, it had become that which shut men out from the law."[44]

Jesus almost ruthlessly put aside the scribes' traditions; yet He religiously lived within the sphere of the Law. Thus, Jesus became the target of the scribes' constant antagonism.

In spite of this, Jesus used this mental image of the scribes to illustrate a new potential for those who would understand the Kingdom of God. Do you tremble at this? It is an occupation called forth by our Lord Jesus Christ Himself — a scribe who is made a disciple of the Kingdom of Heaven.

Surely you noticed that Jesus asked, "Have you understood *all* these things?" Remember, the word "understand" is from the Greek, meaning *to put together* or *to synthesize.* Jesus used "all" not to suggest perfect memory or total comprehension, but to underline the *balance and proportion* in this teaching.

This was a divine discourse, moving steadily forward and unveiling the different phases and processes of the Kingdom of God in its relationship to eras and history. I believe Jesus' question was as much "Do you understand the order or system of this teaching?" as it was "Can you summarize this information?"

I grieve that even great scholars come to Matthew 13 without clarity concerning the chosen order or purpose of Jesus' defined teaching in this setting. Without that understanding, they critically dissect the individual parables, barely mentioning the line-upon-line direction of our Lord here.

But what of that? Or, if we want to ask the real harmonizing question here, "What of *us?*" *Jesus' specific explanation of this parable of the wheat and tares is the clearest statement in the Bible of the true believer's relationship to the world.* An understanding of this statement would immediately save our Christian institutions from our often organized and well-financed plans to alter the battle itself.

This short summary is to prepare us for the storm that may come from one look at Jesus' interpretation. *It is presented out of order in Jesus' discussion* so the explanation will relate most closely to the actual parable for us. But let us not forget that Jesus gave only the parable to the multitude; the explanation was reserved for the disciples alone in a later teaching within the house.

# 13  YOU'RE WHERE YOU'RE SUPPOSED TO BE – IN THE WORLD!

Donald B. Kraybill, whose entire book *The Upside-Down Kingdom* speaks about the truly revolutionary nature of God's Kingdom, writes specifically regarding Jesus' words in Matthew 5:20:

> The ones who work so hard to apply the Torah to everyday life are left behind. Their fervor and enthusiasm for ceremonial piety thwarts God's law of love. *Those who fought so hard for religion are in jeopardy.* The newcomers meanwhile are a motley-looking and irreverent crew, but their righteousness exceeds the righteousness of the Pharisees. [45]

The Scriptures tell us that when the chief priests and the Pharisees heard Jesus' parables, they perceived that He was speaking *about them* (Matt. 21:45,46; Mark 12:12; Luke 20:19). Matthew 13 is no exception. Although not mentioned specifically, we know the status quo was well represented in the multitude Jesus frequently pinpointed as He revealed the tension between the new wine of the Kingdom and the old religious wineskins. Again, Kraybill makes this comparison undeniably real:

What does all this mean for us today? How do Kingdom and church intersect? Jesus described the inbreeding of the Kingdom with two stories (Mark 2:21,22). Always wash a patch before sewing it on an old garment. Otherwise the patch will shrink after the first laundering and rip the old cloth worse than ever. Moreover, store new, fermenting wine in new and flexible wineskins. "Bubbling" wine poured into brittle old skins will crack them open and drain away. The wine is the essential, primary substance. The skins are secondary. We can't drink them, but we do need them to store the wine.[46]

This describes the conflict. *It is a conflict of understanding.* An institution can easily interpret Jesus' parable of the wheat and tares as an illustration concerning disunity in an institutional church. Alexander Maclaren, however, remarks to the contrary:

> The Kingdom of heaven is not a synonym for the church. *Is it not an anachronism to find the church in the parable at all?* No doubt tares are in the church and the parable has a bearing on it, but its primary lesson seems to me to be much wider, and to reveal the conditions of the growth of the Kingdom in human society. [47]

Jesus is consistently pointing us to realize a mission purpose beyond Israel and beyond the Church. That makes this parable even more strategic and its interpretation even more potentially dangerous.

## The Question of the Kingdom: Who Is Lord?

Perhaps that is why it seems easier to start preaching and interpreting the parable before we ever turn to Jesus' interpretation for understanding. After all, we face that temptation in only two of the seven parables where the Master Teacher Himself explains them! Let us hear *Him*, the King Himself.

> Then Jesus sent the multitude away and went into the house. And His disciples came to Him, saying, "Explain to us the parable of the tares of the field."
>
> He answered and said to them: "He who sows the good seed is the Son of Man."

Matthew 13:36,37

Here, as in many parables, the details of the parable alert us to key images that in the Old Testament applied exclusively to God or occasionally to the Messiah and now stand for Jesus Himself. *Here Jesus is the One who both sows the good seed (v. 37) and directs the harvest.*

Philip B. Payne, writing in the *Trinity Journal,* mentions other Old Testament images that Jesus used in His parables to refer to Himself, including *rock, lord,* and *king.* Payne's article title itself says it all: "Jesus' Implicit Claim to Deity in His Parables."[48]

Already mentioned is Brad Young's book that provides some totally different and controversial ties between Jesus' parables and their Jewish rabbinical counterparts. Young argues for a specific issue in our current reference, maintaining that the Kingdom of Heaven is *not* an eschatological concept *but a technical term Jesus employed to speak of God's reign as a present reality* among those who have accepted the call to fulfill the divine purpose.[49]

I refer to both of these to simply emphasize an important foundational understanding from the parable of the wheat and the tares. It is this: *Jesus Christ is owner of the field and steward of the harvest.* It follows, then, that this parable is talking about *a current, present reality and not simply a hoped-for eventuality.*

The question of the Kingdom, of course, is Lordship, or authority. We can't begin to operate fully in God's purpose without a deep, settled understanding that Jesus Christ is Lord. Applying and living out that truth where we have been sowed is *discipleship.* Living it out in our age or era is *influence.*

## The Focus of Divine
## Ownership: The World

Having established ownership, we still struggle until we grasp the focus of this divine ownership. Is it Israel? Is it the Church? *The focus of divine authority and ownership is the world*, not simply any specific arena within the world! As Psalm 24:1 (*KJV*) says, *"The earth is the Lord's and the fulness thereof; the world, and they that dwell therein."* The field is His field, and Jesus' own interpretation in Matthew 13:38 tells us that *"the field is the world...."*

At this point, we must stress that this "world" is not *aion*, meaning *era or age*, but *cosmos* — *the whole of the ordered universe*, including the earth, its inhabitants, and all of creation.

This definitely needs more emphasis, for it is an understanding that changes everything, Ray Stedman writes, "It is essential to notice that the field represents *not* the church but *the world. These sons of the kingdom are put where God wants them — in the world."*[50]

In a longer and more detailed manner, Alexander Maclaren wrote along this same line many years ago:

> Whatever view we take of the bearing of this parable on purity of communion in the visible Church, *we should not slur over Christ's own explanation of 'the field,' lest we miss the lesson that He claims the whole world as His, and contemplates the sowing of the seed broadcast over it all. The Kingdom of Heaven is to be developed on, and to spread through, the whole earth. The world belongs to Christ not only when it is filled with the kingdom, but before the sowing.*[51]

We cannot miss "the lesson" as Maclaren calls it: Christ wishes the sowing of seed to be broadcast over all the world. But what's more, "the world belongs to Christ...[even] before the sowing."

One writer deliberates that the tenses of both verbs in *"...The kingdom of heaven is LIKE* [or likened to] *a man who SOWED good seed"* (v. 24) *shows that the Kingdom is concentrated in Him* by the already accomplished act of His sowing. G. Campbell Morgan writes, "Our toil and conflict are directed rather toward bringing back to the rightful owner that which belongs to Him."[52]

Again we hear from Maclaren on this matter: "Our Lord veils His claims by speaking of the sower in the third person; but the hearing ear cannot fail to catch the implication throughout that He Himself is the sower and the Lord of the harvest. The field is 'his field,' and His own interpretation tells us that *it means the world*."[53]

Exactly how does this affect us? If we grasp that this mission reaches beyond the Church and beyond Israel, how will we be changed? What phenomenal attitude adjustment will alter our focus, our labor, and our prayer?

In an emotional response to these questions, one writer answers as follows:

> I find in these facts a conviction which sends me out upon the track of His feet to serve and to suffer, and to share the travail which makes His Kingdom come. *Everything belongs to Him, mountains and valleys, continents and countries, beasts and birds, flowers and fruits and men of all kindred and tribes and nations. The recognition of this fundamental fact is necessary to the interpretation of the parable. The great Kingdom of Jesus is far from its perfect order, but no other than He has any crown rights throughout the whole world.*[54]

How can we fail to grasp this thought as we are sent out upon the track where Jesus' feet walked before us? We are working to establish His "crown rights."

Please allow me one very contemporary application of this truth:

> Wherever you are, as a child of God, as a son of the Kingdom by faith in Jesus Christ, you have been put there by the Lord Jesus. It is so important to understand that He has *sown you and put you where you are*. The church, you see, is to gather together for worship, for instruction, and for

mutual fellowship, but then it is to go out. There is a kind of rhythm of life within the church — it comes *together*, then goes out again, scattered out into the world. And where you are out there is where the word of witness is given, where the truth of the word is promulgated. That is what the Lord has in mind here. The field therefore is the world, the human race, society, as we normally term it. *In that world of humanity the Lord Jesus has scattered His own.*[55]

Therefore, we bow before the Lord's answer — the focus of divine authority and ownership is *the world*. To this end we, too, must accordingly direct our lives, our work, and our expectation.

# 14 DON'T TOIL OVER TARES

C an this be doubted? The primary purpose of this second interpreted parable in Jesus' set discourse on the Kingdom of God is to teach the *conduct* of the King (and thus of His loyal subjects) as it pertains *to the growth of the tares*. I want to cry out, "Eureka!" That's an issue that consistently plagues sincere Christians and their related institutions.

## Understanding God's 'Game Plan'

We have marked carefully from the first parable the plan of the owner to sow believers throughout the world with an expectation of influence on the age in which they live. Now we are shown clearly that *it is the strategy and product both of God's Kingdom and of the enemy to sow people into each age of history, thus incarnating principle through individuals.*

Read again Matthew 13:38: *"The field is the world, the good seeds are the sons of the kingdom, but the tares are the sons of the wicked one."* Hold this thought clearly in your mind as you consider this: The game of soccer or football proceeds through a tightly enforced set of rules and procedures. In the same way, there must be a clear game plan in the church.

Unless the believer clearly understands the true strategy, much of his energy and devotion, although sincere and often sacrificial, can become misdirected. He simply doesn't know the territory. As Alexander Maclaren writes:

> Men become children of the kingdom by taking the Gospel into their hearts, and thereby receive a new principle of growth, which in truth becomes themselves. Side by side with the sower's beneficent work the counter-working of "his enemy" goes on. As the one, by depositing holy truth in the heart, makes men "children of the kingdom," the other, by putting evil principles therein, makes men "children of evil." [56]

Our required understanding at this point is *a restatement of the value of all mankind.* People are the objects in this ultimate purpose. With this, of course, comes a shuddering reality — the infinite outcome of humanity's choices. Indeed, there *is* no neutrality; rather, all men and women become themselves players.

## The Enemy's Strategy To Sow Tares

We have already pointed out that Jesus in both the parable of the tares and the parable of the dragnet focuses uncomfortably (for many) on everlasting punishment. But that end must be first seen through the personal antagonist to Christ and His purpose. *"An enemy has done this...,"* the field owner declares in the parable itself (v. 28). *"The enemy who sowed them is the devil..."* Jesus explains in His commentary (v. 39).

After saying that the lesson of this parable is one of the most amazing in Jesus' repertoire, William Barclay goes on to write:

> It teaches us that there is always a hostile power in the world, seeking and waiting to destroy the good seed. Our experience of life is that both kinds of influence act upon our lives, the influence which will help the seed of the word to flourish and to grow, and *the influence which will seek to*

*destroy the good seed, before it can produce fruit at all.* It is the lesson of life that we must be forever on our guard. [57]

On our guard, indeed! We know that there is a real, personal adversary. The word "devil" (*diablos*) means exactly that: *an adversary.* Therefore, we must understand his purpose and be forever vigilant.

The consequences are so real. Why, then, as the Church age lengthens, do we seem to doubt more and more the sure and real consummation (*harvest*) of the age and of mankind's choices? Why does the subject of eternal consequences stagger our understanding? We must clearly hear Jesus on this issue, or the rest of the subject blurs into insignificance.

"The enemy who sowed them is the devil, the harvest is the end of the age, and the reapers are the angels.

"Therefore as the tares are gathered and burned in the fire, so it will be at the end of this age.

"The Son of Man will send out His angels, and they will gather out of His kingdom all things that offend, and those who practice lawlessness,

"and will cast them into the furnace of fire. There will be wailing and gnashing of teeth.

"Then the righteous will shine forth as the sun in the kingdom of their Father. He who has ears to hear, let him hear!

Matthew 13:39-43

Barclay, sometimes criticized but ever desirous that the *average* Christian clearly understand the Word, writes the following:

It teaches us that judgment does come in the end. *Judgment is not hasty, but judgment does come.* The separation of the good and the bad *does come* in the end. It may be that, humanly speaking, in this life the sinner seems to escape the consequences, but there is a life to come. It may be that, humanly speaking, goodness never seems to enter into its reward, but there is a new world to redress the balance of the old. [58]

But most amazing of all to me is that the tares are gathered out of Christ's Kingdom. In other words, the field of the world will then indeed become the Kingdom of Christ.

## The Ultimate End of the Tares

It is clear there is a division even among the tares themselves, between *"all things that offend, and those who practice lawlessness"* (v. 41). One writer adds, "There are two classes among the tares: men whose evil has been a snare to others (for the 'things that offend' must, in accordance with the context, be taken to be persons), and the *less* guilty, who are simply called 'them that do iniquity.'"[59]

Even more specifically in the original parable are these words: *"...First gather together the tares and bind them in bundles to burn them, but gather the wheat into my barn"* (v. 30). From the beginning of the Church era has been the suggestion that there may be in eternity "assortment according to sin." No one can forget this illustration in Dante's circles of hell.

Jesus, I believe, implies this in teaching that some will be beaten with few stripes and some with many stripes. Maclaren remarks, "What a bond of fellowship that would be."[60]

Clearly the reward of believers will mark a separation by faithfulness and thus eternal purpose. Is that also true here? Alexander Maclaren, in one of the most specific yet succinct statements I have ever read on the judgment at the end of the age writes this:

At the consummation of the allotted era, the *bands of human society are to be dissolved, and a new principle of association is to determine men's place.* Their moral and religious *affinities* will bind them together or separate them, and all other ties will snap. This marshalling according to religious character is *the main thought of the solemn closing words* of the parable and of its interpretation, in which our Lord presents Himself as directing the whole process of judgment by means of the "angels" who execute His commands. They are "His angels," and whatever may be the unknown activity put forth by them in the parting of men, it is all done in obedience to Him. What stupendous claims Jesus makes here! [61]

Can I accept and proclaim this with the urgency the Word demands? Again, Maclaren writes:

"The furnace," as it is emphatically called by eminence, burns up the bundles. We may *freely admit that the fire is part of the parable,* but yet let us *not* forget that it occurs not only in the parable, but *in the interpretation;* and let us learn that the prose *reality of "everlasting destruction," which Christ here solemnly announces, is awful and complete.* For a moment He passes beyond the limits of that parable, to add that terrible clause about *"weeping and gnashing of teeth,"* the tokens of despair and rage. So spoke the most loving and truthful lips. [62]

I will tell you in advance that in the final parable of Jesus' discourse — the parable of the dragnet — He will once more repeat this teaching of the furnace of fire. Once again, Jesus will warn, *"...There will be wailing and gnashing of teeth"* (v. 50).

We would do well to ask ourselves the question that Maclaren asks: *"Do we believe His warnings as well as His promises?"* [63]

# 15   My Father's World

$A$re you ready yet to answer the Master's query, *"...Have you understood ALL these things..."* (v. 51)? It is true that we've tackled only two of the seven parables, and we're not yet finished with the second. You may say the question is premature. Yet as mentioned earlier, these two parables are *fundamental* to the rest.

## Bringing Out the New and the Old

Are you comfortable with what we have already learned? Perhaps we should repeat the promise based on understanding that we can be *"...like a householder who brings out of his treasure things new and old"* (v. 52).

Specifically, this is talking about *possessed* or *laid-up* treasure. *New* does not mean *young* any more than *old* means *worn out*. The reference seems to be to "fresh things" or *application* as contrasted to *ancient or established truth*. Concerning this scripture, Morgan writes:

> The principle is old, the application is new. The root is old, the blossom and the fruit are new, and the two are necessary to growth and development.... "Things new and

101

old" — old in their unseen and eternal principles; new in their seen and temporal practice. The interrelation is for evermore a test. The new thing which contradicts the old is always false. The old thing that has no fresh and new production is dead, and the sooner we are rid of it the better.[64]

So to understand these truths is to be a scribe instructed concerning the Kingdom of Heaven. That puts us in the enviable position of becoming the ruling authorities, capable of bringing this necessary "new and old" application to our age and era.

In a sense, by using the strong Eastern phrase "householder" or "house-despot," Jesus clearly suggests that His disciples are meant to possess a certain mastery for their age, using their understanding (their "treasury") to prepare for Him and to make ready the Kingdom. Remember, all this concerns the conditions of the growth of the Kingdom in human society. Or as G. E. Ladd has reminded us, "...to bring men in the present age the blessings of the messianic age...."

Those who understand the Kingdom bring the finger of God (the Holy Spirit) to the application and remedy of situations in their age. *Here must be for us great conviction and yet wonderful peace.*

## Living as Good Stewards Of This World

May I take the liberty of finishing this parable's discussion with some fragments from my own heart? They are, I believe with some presumption, an example of bringing out new and old to understand and apply Kingdom understanding. The first of these must be obvious. The field (this world) is owned by the Son of Man. We are to *enjoy* it, but at the same time we are also to act as good stewards of it, constantly reminding Satan and his forces to take their hands off that which legally belongs to the Master.

Many assume that the principalities of the age ended up in past eras given to darkness. Perhaps that is true. However, I agree with

102

Morgan and others that the devil left his proper habitation and thus sacrificed his right to his principality. As Morgan states, *"Oh, the comfort of the certainty that the devil has no claim to the world!"*[65]

There can be no doubt that we miss much in our thinking and our work as Christians "...because we have been too ready to yield to him [the devil] as his right everything upon which his hand rests."[66] Instead, our approach should be like any steward: *"Hands off in the name of the owner!"*

Please do not quickly skip through the following words in an attempt to get to the next point. Morgan's message here is crucial to our ability to live as good stewards representing God's Kingdom:

> To me it is as remarkable and valuable a fact that Jesus came to show the work of the devil as that He came to reveal God. Paul could say, "We are not ignorant of his devices," but he could not have said that until he had been brought into the light of the Christian revelation. It is when a man submits himself to Jesus Christ that he sees clearly, not God only, not himself only, but his enemy also. It is one of the great advantages of coming into the light of Christ's teaching that man is enabled to see the devil for what he is, and is able therefore to place a true value on both his person and his purpose.[67]

## Good Seed Sown in the Father's World

Maltbie D. Babcock many years ago wrote a popular hymn:[68]

> This is my Father's world, and to my listening ears
> All nature sings, and 'round me rings,
> the music of the spheres.
> This is my Father's world. I rest me in the thought
> Of rocks and trees, of skies and seas;
> His hand the wonders wrought.

Now, of course, hymns are not even sung by a growing proportion of Christian churches. And even where hymns are sung, the words of Babcock's hymn sound liberal and "New-Age"-oriented. After all, we say, we're interested in souls, *not* creation. The second verse, however, begins to address the issue:

This is my Father's world. The birds their carols raise.
The morning light, the lily white
declare their Maker's praise.
This is my Father's world. He shines in all that's fair.
In the rustling grass *I hear Him pass;*
*He speaks to me ev'rywhere.*

Many Christians have never even heard the phrase "general revelation," or they have relegated it to the heap of inadequacy. Yet Psalm 19 declares unashamedly:

The heavens declare the glory of God; and the firmament shows His handiwork.
Day unto day utters speech, and night unto night reveals knowledge.
There is no speech nor language where their voice is not heard.
Their line has gone out through all the earth, and their words to the end of the world. In them He has set a tabernacle for the sun.

Psalm 19:1-4

Babcock writes, *"In the rustling grass I hear Him pass; He speaks to me everywhere."* What a tragic loss when sullen, legalistic believers reject such thoughts as this, committing themselves instead to accept only limited expressions of the divine voice! But I must hasten on. Read carefully Babcock's final verse:

This is my Father's world. O let me ne'er forget
That tho' the wrong seems oft so strong,
*God is the ruler yet.*
This is my Father's world. *The battle is not done;*

104

Jesus, who died, *shall be satisfied,*
*And earth and heav'n be one.*

Remember, the Christian who knows God's program will choose to intelligently cooperate with God's purpose for the believer and the church in this era. Christians *are* good seed sown into the Father's world.

We are on this earth to produce fruit, planted in the midst of an age that is against the King, yet exerting an influence that will tell for the King. We are good seed sown in the Father's world, and we must grow where we are planted!

G. Campbell Morgan wrote the following in his marvelous old English:

> Wherever sorrow is assuaged, where wounds are healed, where love becomes the law of life, wherever men are loosed from the power of sin, there the Kingdom of God is come. And such harvest is the result of the living seeds flung from the hands of the living Sower upon the soil.[69]

Perhaps you find yourself agreeing with this last application as you think through the hymn and the psalm to find personal peace and confident expression.

## Leave the Tares Alone

But a more dangerous conclusion lies ahead. *When it came to the tares, the Master said, "Let it alone."*

It is impossible to distinguish between wheat and tares when they are mingled — those in the Kingdom versus those who are not. Again, the Master is clear in His message, which in essence says, "Don't worry about sorting them out! God's angels are ready to bundle them up at the end of the age."

*Well enough,* you think. But does your heart agree?

It has appeared to me in recent years that a significant amount of evangelical energy has been devoted to tearing out the tares from the midst of society. As a result, the work of many Christians has appeared to be angry and hostile to observers in the world; their very rebukes seem oriented toward judgment and condemnation.

There is no need here to name specific issues and possibly cause defensiveness on the part of the reader. Suffice it to say that our Master predicted that the destruction of true wheat would inevitably result whenever Christians attempted to prematurely separate or eliminate the tares.

Many of us certainly appeared more as tares than as wheat at some stage of our lives. Spiritually speaking, however, what appear to be tares are often wheat. This is why premature judgment and divisive action will always produce destruction. I cannot make this more personal.

Again, Morgan articulates our conclusion:

> As to the sowing, there is a phrase which we must not miss, "*among the wheat.*" This does not necessarily mean that all who are not Christian people are to be described as darnel. The word "among" has behind it two Greek words. One of these words would suffice for ordinary expression, but the combination of the two lends intensity to the thought. The phrase occurs only four times in the New Testament, once used here, again by Mark in connection with the same teaching, again in the Corinthian letter in quite another realm of thought, and once more in Revelation, where it is said that the Lamb is "in the midst of the throne." It is the most intense way of saying "among." Herein is revealed the subtlety of the foe. He scattered his darnel *among* the wheat. The devil's method is that of *mingling the counterfeit with the real.* It is that of *introducing into the Master's own property that which is so like the good that at first you cannot tell the difference.* That is the devil's mission of imitation. It is the heart of the parable.[70]

Please continue to note that Morgan's statement applies to the agreed-upon sowing — namely, in the world. *So this false and intimate sowing of the devil is "in the world," not in the church.*

Even a small agreement with what has been discovered about Jesus' decisive direction concerning the tares sends us into the world with compassion and hopefulness as representatives of the Kingdom. We recognize, of course, that Satan's method in this age is *imitation* — mingling the counterfeit with the real. But with prayerful discernment, we need be neither gullible nor destructive. When we know the genuine, we will seldom fall for the counterfeit. Instead, our Kingdom faith will be filled with the hopefulness and power of the Holy Spirit, for we believe that every person and situation is open to the effect of the Kingdom of Heaven.

## The Kingdom Attitude
## Of Humility and Hope

Some scholars even teach that "Kingdom of Heaven" is a more specific term that refers to attitudes, dispositions, and lifestyles from the ultimate Kingdom that are then applied to one's family, work situation, and life-affirming expectations. I'm not sure I understand such a division of terms, but I understand the principle!

An earlier quote reminded us that Kingdom folk influence the age by both recognizing and approximating the government of God. It is practically the entire thesis of Kraybill's book, quoted earlier, that the Kingdom changes one's lifestyle. One of his conclusions is particularly applicable:

> The corporate life of the people of God will be visible and external. These are the folk who engage in conspicuous sharing. We practice Jubilee. Generosity replaces consumption and accumulation. Our faith wags our pocketbook. We give without expecting a return. We forgive liberally as God forgave us. We overlook the signs of stigma hanging from the unlovely. Genuine compassion for the poor and destitute

move us. We look and move down the ladder. We don't take our own religious structure too seriously; we know Jesus is Lord and Master of religious custom. We serve instead of dominate. We prefer invitation over force.[71]

So Kingdom people live out a little bit of Heaven upon earth. When they pray, "Thy Kingdom come, Thy will be done on earth as it is in heaven," *they believe it*!

There is humility to this in practice. We know that no one who only sees in part (such as ourselves) can judge the whole. We also know that although mingled during growth, tares can only be separated in maturity. Love, never hate and judgment, is our Kingdom personality. We even love our enemies, and revenge is a *non sequitur*.

Kraybill writes, *"Generosity, Jubilee, mercy, compassion — these are the marks of the new community."*[72] And again, he stresses, *"We're citizens of a future that is already breaking in."*[73]

The spirit of Jesus has always been one of patient hope and of awaiting the development of the inner truth. We see that quality as He rescues the woman taken in adultery or meets by night with Nicodemus. It is also manifested when Jesus accepts a prostitute's offering of a broken alabaster box; freely goes home to dine with the tax collector Zacchaeus; or touches lepers, even when it means that not only *He* will be quarantined and condemned, but His village will be as well.

What brave and courageous action it must take to reject what Kraybill calls the "right-side-up kingdom" in order to embrace the "upside-down agenda." Yet it will work; it *does* work. It is, as we have seen, an "already but not yet" Kingdom, a future that is already breaking into society.

The "rent-a-mob" in Thessalonica cried out to the rulers with tears of rage, *"...These who have turned the world upside down have come here too."* When they later added, *"...saying there is another king —*

*Jesus"* (Acts 17:6,7), they spoke what we should treasure as a compliment, not flee from as criticism.

We *do* purpose a turnaround in society through a Kingdom revolution. But our purpose as Kingdom people is certainly the reverse of man's political expectation. The decrees of this Kingdom mirror the compassion found in the lifestyle of its King.

Jesus was perhaps the last believer on the world's party list. During the time He walked on this earth, He endeared Himself both to the children and to the weak and powerless of the world. Now we are His seed, the incarnate truth of His Kingdom. As we go out into this world, we are to gladly endorse and model His behavior, bringing the blessings of the Messianic Kingdom to the men and women of this age.

# 16 MUSTARD SEED AND LEAVEN

"This is my Father's world" — this is our Father's *church*. Jesus is Lord, and we're committed to His Kingdom. But are we literal in that commitment? I heard many years ago four questions we should ask ourselves to determine how well we are doing in our commitment to the Kingdom of God.

1. What kind of a Christian do we want to release into the world? What does he look like? How does he respond? (The Christian in the world, after all, is our final product!)

2. What kind of a church produces that kind of Christian? (Family genes run strong in both the physical abilities of a life and its potential to disease. Similarly, we release what we produce in our fellowship, whether good or bad.)

3. What kind of leadership (board, elders, and so forth) enables that kind of church to produce *that* kind of Christian? (Not an insignificant detail! Leadership envisions or destroys — the power of life and death is often in their hands.)

4. Finally (at least in my sequence), what kind of pastoral leadership develops and empowers that kind of shared leadership, so they can in turn empower and develop that kind of church?

I truly believe that Matthew 13 is a battle plan; on the other hand, it is also a careful checklist for the significant task of producing and releasing a certain type of living seed into the world. Jesus calls these parables "mysteries of the kingdom of heaven" (Matt. 13:11). He has shared these secrets with us and told us how our understanding will work.

> "For whoever has, to him more will be given, and he will have abundance; but whoever does not have, even what he has will be taken away from him."
>
> Matthew 13:12

In other words, if you get a grip on part of these truths — these secrets of Christ's Kingdom — you will find yourself being led into more and more understanding.

I think the next two parables are particularly good examples of this principle. They are the last teaching Jesus gives to the multitude before going into the house with the disciples and concluding His single discourse with them alone.

The evangelist adds his meaning as Jesus sends the multitude away:

> All these things Jesus spoke to the multitude in parables; and without a parable He did not speak to them,
> that it might be fulfilled which was spoken by the prophet, saying: "I will open My mouth in parables; I will utter things kept secret from the foundation of the world."
>
> Matthew 13:34,35

This quote is actually from Psalm 78, attributed as a "maskil" or a wisdom teaching of Asaph, who was David's chief musician, worship leader, and psalmist. Obviously from this reference, Asaph was a *prophetic* musician!

## Unlikely Symbols
## Of the Kingdom of Heaven

I believe these last two parables in the multitude portion of Jesus' teaching are a unit — the parables of the mustard seed and the leaven. But regardless of how these parables are taken, they both cast a tremendous light on vital issues of the Kingdom.

The words of our Lord continue:

> Another parable He put forth to them, saying: "The kingdom of heaven is like a mustard seed, which a man took and sowed in his field,
> "which indeed is the least of all the seeds; but when it is grown it is greater than the herbs and becomes a tree, so that the birds of the air come and nest in its branches."
>
> Matthew 13:31,32

For whatever reason, Jesus does not give an interpretation to these two parables. However, we have already learned from Jesus' words what the field is, what the seed represents, who the enemy is, and the nature of God's strategy. The essential truth, however, is that *"...the good seed are the sons of the kingdom"* (Matt. 13:38).

In the parable of the mustard seed, there are five symbols: the sower (again); the field (again); the seed (in this case, the mustard seed); the tree that grows from the seed; and the birds that make their nests in the tree.

Let's observe as well the second parable of this set and see if the two are not attached.

> Another parable He spoke to them: "The kingdom of heaven is like leaven, which a woman took and hid in three measures of meal till it was all leavened."
>
> Matthew 13:33

Here are two incredible symbols in Jesus' Kingdom teaching. Again, let us take note that these parables were to unfold mysteries

113

and secrets of the age between the first coming and the second coming of the Messiah — between the Kingdom already and the Kingdom not yet, the Kingdom "here and now" and the Kingdom "then and there."

Every element of these parables discloses some factor of movement in history about the Kingdom of God. They *are* wise sayings, but they are also dark sayings. They *can* be understood, my dear friend, but only by the sincere. The critical simply find further darkness.

Perhaps you have seen a popular new gimmick in theaters where the actors present the story or the play, and then they let the audience decide, from several options, the way the story should end.

Personally, I am not generally known for indecision. People have seldom accused me of not speaking my mind or leaving folks in the dark as to where I stand on any subject! But there are elements in these parables that present major classical options. I actually think we should hear the various opinions to truly discover their impact.

You remember that Jesus often used the same parable or illustration in totally different settings. Do you suppose He wanted us to see more than one, or even several, possibilities in these parables? Could the mustard seed and the leaven represent more than one concept? Are they meant to suggest more than one scenario and lead to more than one conclusion and application? I believe this is very possible.

First, all scholars agree that mustard seed and leaven are both *unlikely* symbols for the Kingdom of Heaven. One writer calls them "bizarre and incongruous."[74] For example, everyone knows that yeast normally symbolizes evil. Doesn't it?

Barclay says, "Jesus chose this so that people hearing about the kingdom of God would be shocked when it's compared to leaven, and the shock would arouse their interest, and rivet their attention as an illustration of an unusual unexpected nature."[75]

114

Certainly in both these parables, the strange choice of image evokes surprise. They encourage the reader to penetrate the parable's meaning. They seem designed to jar the unthinking about the coming of the Kingdom of God.

## Interpreting the Mustard Seed

And why did Jesus choose the image of a mustard seed? It really isn't the smallest of all seeds in the Middle East. That would be the cypress. And, by the way, *that* particular "smallest of all seeds" does indeed produce a truly legitimate tree — the cypress tree. The mustard seed, however, had come to be known among the Jews. It was a more common illustration in Hebrew thinking of something very small.

I'm sure you have also asked the question, "Does the mustard seed ever produce a tree?" Not exactly! About the best you get is a large shrub, which can grow ten or twelve feet tall. Now, birds do indeed flock to this shrub, but it really doesn't become a tree! Something abnormal seems afoot in what Jesus says in this proverb about the mustard seed.

Let's look at some classical interpretations that are worth reviewing. First, William Barclay writes:

> The point of this parable is crystal clear. The kingdom of heaven starts from the smallest beginning but no man knows where it will end. The kingdom of heaven starts with the smallest of beginnings and great things happen as it goes on.[76]

Another study teaches the following:

> The mustard is the smallest seed, one of the smallest seeds of the garden, but in Palestine frequently produced the plant which grew 12 feet in height. This was a story of encouragement for disciples and early Christians and for us now. The Jews had expected the kingdom of God to come

with awesome spectacle, not from a baby boy, and a suffering Savior.[77]

That last sentence bears repeating! The author continues:

> Jesus encouraged the twelve disciples with the truth. The kingdom of God would exceed its humble beginnings around the Sea of Galilee and those same humble beginnings would produce a faith that spread rapidly and influence the world for almost 2000 years.[78]

Now, I can really see this author's point in the context of Matthew 13. As we have seen, hatred was beginning to develop against Jesus, as well as opposition and criticism against the disciples.

Another writer says, "Instead, the point is the organic unity of small beginnings and mature end." What he says next is very important, so let us read on:

> It's really not so much the greatness of the end; everybody could understand the kingdom would eventually be this, but it has to do with small beginnings. No pious Jew doubted that the kingdom was coming glorious. What Jesus is teaching goes beyond that. He is saying there is *a connection between small beginnings taking place under the ministry and the kingdom eventually in its future glory.* Though the initial appearance of the kingdom may seem inconsequential, the tiny seed leads to the mature plant.[79]

Perhaps these words help us see why Jesus chose the mustard seed. At this moment, He was not stressing the greatness of a future Kingdom; few would dispute that. Rather, it was more important for Him to find a metaphor to emphasize the Kingdom's tiny beginning. I think that is a very important word and deeply applicable to this study.

But just a moment. Perhaps Jesus isn't showing a *good* picture at all! Perhaps this parable is about an *unnatural* development in the future Kingdom.

Some time ago, Ray Stedman, a neighboring pastor and teacher, shared his feelings in a message called "The Case of the Ambitious Seed." He believes that Jesus is actually showing in this parable that His Kingdom might experience abnormal growth — growth that was contrary to His purpose. For example, instead of simplicity and servanthood, the church might produce grandeur, greatness, and hierarchy — something that was never God's intent at all.

There is an amazing parallel between that way of thinking and the words of G. Campbell Morgan, who wrote almost a century earlier. The world isn't seeing the Kingdom of God yet. In fact, Morgan says, "We talk very glibly about Christian nations; but there are no Christian nations."[80] We can certainly say that today, can't we? Regardless of its prominence in this particular age, no modern nation can be called a Christian nation.

Both Stedman and Morgan see the mustard seed's growth into a tree as an abnormal process and an unintended direction. If they are correct, could the branches of the tree represent the many divisions in the Kingdom? Could the birds represent that which takes the truth of the Gospel away from its simplicity? It's a worthy thought to consider.

## The Symbol of the Leaven

What then is the leaven? The majority of teachers positively translate Jesus' parable of the leaven and the flour. Again, let's examine a couple of these interpretations. A previously quoted home study includes these words:

> This story illustrates how the Christian message will spread throughout the entire world. It will change everything it touches with revolutionary force — people, social orders, economic relations, and, finally, the purpose of

history. Because of Jesus, the world will never be the same again. Our hospitals, colleges and universities, our judicial systems, and our agencies for alleviating human need and suffering are all traceable to the small beginnings of Jesus' ministry in Galilee and Palestine.[81]

Barclay writes the following regarding this parable:

The whole point of this parable lies in one thing, it's the transforming power of leaven. Unleavened bread, bread baked without leaven is like a water biscuit, hard, and dry, and unappetizing and non-interesting. But bread baked with leaven is soft, and porous, and spongy, and tasty. The introduction of the leaven causes a transformation in the dough and the coming of the kingdom causes a transformation in life.[82]

Specifically, Jesus said, *"...The kingdom of heaven is like leaven, which a woman took and hid in three measures of meal till it was all leavened"* (v. 33). What are three measures? The Greek word for "measure" is *sata*, three of which measured approximately two pecks. *That's a bushel of flour*, equivalent to 128 cups! With 42 or so cups of water added, you would have 101 pounds of dough on your hands! As one writer says, "This is no slip of a girl making two tiny loaves for her husband's pleasure. This is a *baker*, folks!"[83]

That same writer, Robert Capon, continues:

Which leads me, as long as we're at the end of the parable anyway, to exegete it backwards. Take the "whole" first. When Jesus says the *whole* is leavened, he's not kidding. The lump stands for the whole world. It's not some elite ball of brioche dough made out of some fancy flour by special handling. And it's not some hyper-good-for-you chunk thoughts, or spiritual fad bread full of soy flour, wheat germ, and pure thoughts. It's just plain, unbaked bread dough, and Jesus postulates enough of it to make it even handle like the plain old world it represents: that is, *not easily*. Indigestible in its present form, incapable of going anywhere, either to heaven or hell, except in a handbasket — and absolutely certain to wear out anybody, God included, who tries to handle it — it is, if we dare rate such things, one of Jesus' parabolic triumphs: a perfect 100+, if there ever was one.[84]

Certainly these are interesting comments about a mysterious parable. On the other hand, leaven in the Bible inevitably represents that which is evil.

You may remember the account in Matthew 16 of a boat trip Jesus took with His disciples on the Sea of Galilee. The disciples were worried about not having any bread to eat, but Jesus was concerned about something far more important.

> Then Jesus said to them, "Take heed and beware of the leaven of the Pharisees and the Sadducees."
> And they reasoned among themselves, saying, "It is because we have taken no bread."
> But Jesus, being aware of it, said to them, "O you of little faith, why do you reason among yourselves because you have brought no bread?
> "Do you not yet understand, or remember the five loaves of the five thousand and how many baskets you took up?
> "Nor the seven loaves of the four thousand and how many large baskets you took up?
> "How is it you do not understand that I did not speak to you concerning bread? — but to beware of the leaven of the Pharisees and Sadducees."
> Then they understood that He did not tell them to beware of the leaven of bread, but of the doctrine of the Pharisees and Sadducees.
>
> Matthew 16:6-12

In this case, Jesus used the image of leaven to represent a ritualistic, legalistic, materialistic type of religion.

Look now in First Corinthians. The following passage has to do with the incestuous relationship of a young man in the church and the fact that the church was not judging it. Paul writes in the fifth chapter:

> Your glorying is not good. Do you not know that a little leaven leavens the whole lump?
> Therefore purge out the old leaven, that you may be a new lump, since you truly are unleavened. For indeed Christ, our Passover, was sacrificed for us.
> Therefore let us keep the feast, not with old leaven, *nor with the leaven of malice and wickedness,* but with the unleavened bread of sincerity and truth.
>
> 1 Corinthians 5:6-8

The same concept is given by Paul in Galatians:

> You have become estranged from Christ, you who attempt to be justified by law; you have fallen from grace.
> For we through the Spirit eagerly wait for the hope of righteousness by faith.
> For in Christ Jesus neither circumcision nor uncircumcision avails anything, but faith working through love.
> You ran well. Who hindered you from obeying the truth?
> This persuasion does not come from Him who calls you.
> *A little leaven leavens the whole lump.*
>
> Galatians 5:4-9

So in a sense, the New Testament frame of reference suggests to us that leaven is not a positive picture. Perhaps Jesus was saying in this Matthew 13 teaching that a mixture would come in the Kingdom of God that was never meant to be there. Certainly it is difficult to trace the roots of institutional religion's pomp and grandeur back to the simplicity that Jesus taught!

God's Kingdom was never meant to be a place where positions are sought and ambition is promoted. Today it's difficult to find examples of Jesus' teaching: "You must be a servant of all." Indeed, a significant measure of leaven has been added to the mix!

In truth, however, the Bible also presents an outstanding picture of the positive use of leaven, both in Leviticus 7:13 and again in Leviticus 23:17. The Leviticus 23 passage concerns the Feast of Pentecost, or the Feast of Weeks. This festival included a new meal offering, which was to consist of two loaves of bread baked in the people's homes and brought to the priest to present before the Lord. *However, these two loaves of bread were to have leaven in them!*

Was this the Holy Spirit's way of saying, "I know that when the church is instituted, it will consist of people who are not perfect"? This picture certainly presents some interesting possibilities!

So we see that dichotomies exist in the parables of the mustard seed and of leaven. Jesus gives us no help in interpreting these parables. However, they are placed in a tightly woven single discourse, and that context helps us immeasurably.

Perhaps at the moment Jesus taught these parables, He really did simply want to give us direction and stir our awareness concerning the operation of God's Kingdom in light of His upcoming physical absence from the world. Then again, perhaps the conclusions are the most important truths for us to understand.

You see, mustard seed has a side to it that Jesus' listeners would have immediately recognized and that no one would have doubted. As one writer points out, "Mustard has the quality of pungency. It is biting, irritating, disturbing...."[85] Perhaps this is what the Lord most wanted us to remember.

# Worldwide Change – One Person At a Time

# 17

The family in which I was raised only considered medical doctors as a last resort. They possessed a strong belief in God's commitment to healing and, in addition, knew of a plethora of simple home remedies.

For instance, if anyone admitted to a cough or flu, my mother was quick to prepare a mustard plaster. And what is that, you ask? Mom would pour dry mustard on a warm towel or other piece of cloth; then she would wet and again warm the towel. When that mixture was placed on one's chest, it produced a *serious* heat. In fact, I think that may be what happened to my chest hair! Why fear hell when I could fear mustard plaster? It seemed much more immediate and sure!

## The Power To Change an Era

Here is how one writer expresses a similar story:

The influence and working of the kingdom is a violent disturbing force, plain for all to see. When Christians came to Thessalonika the cry was, those who have turned the world upside down have come here. The action of

Christianity is disruptive, disturbing, violent in its effect. It's true that men crucified Jesus Christ because He disturbed their orthodox habits and conventions. And again and again it has been true that Christianity has been persecuted because it desires to take both men and society and to remake them. It's abundantly clear that there is nothing in this world so disturbing as Christianity, and in fact it is the reason why so many people hate it, resent it, refuse it, and would wish to eliminate it.[86]

Was this one of the principles Jesus was asking us to understand? The Kingdom of God will produce an ultimate consequence that is out of all proportion to its beginning. Mustard seed does not suggest thermonuclear power, but rather *extraordinary, pungent power*. Like leaven, which works silently, the Kingdom of God begins with the smallest silent influences, yet eventually changes the ultimate composition of an era.

The church where I served for thirty years as a senior pastor is a great example of this. It began with women meeting together in a prayer meeting; later it became a small church around a coal fire. Within that tiny church were a few women to whom God had spoken, telling them that the church would have worldwide impact and influence and that it would be both a filling station and a sending center.

Little could these women have imagined the ultimate results of that prophetic word. They sent their first missionary, Flora Colby, as a medical missionary to Lebanon. From that point on, they began investing themselves into the world and the future. A great number of mission fields have literally been opened through their faith and sacrifice.

Both parables have another obvious and similar understanding. Both the smallness of the mustard seed and the silence of leaven tell us that in order to find the Kingdom of God in any era, we have to reject society's view of bigness and success; instead, we must look for *the power of transformation* in the penetration of individuals and the day of small beginnings. It is there that we will find the Kingdom.

God produces worldwide change, one person at a time. And, of course, as we have said, side by side with the Sower's beneficial work is the counterwork of His enemy. One deposits holy truth in the heart, causing people to become children of His Kingdom; the other plants evil principles within men, making them children of destruction.

We must realize that God brings forth fruit for His Kingdom from small and inconsequential beginnings in our personal lives as well. When God begins His work of change in our lives, He often deals in *micro*-change, even though we sometimes ask for, demand, and expect *macro*-change. We are, however, often unwilling to start, so God will start His work in us in many infinitely small and seemingly unnoticed ways.

## The Other Side

Let me also say that the history of the Christian church shows unquestioning compromise with abnormal growth and false leavening influences. We cannot study these parables, nor can we study the Scriptures, without knowing that the truth and sincerity of the Gospel will constantly be under attack by both compromise and change.

So, too, it is in our lives. We start out with simple, pure, honest, and absolutely sincere direction; then it begins to change. The Kingdom of God works unseen, transforming without pomp or display. The silent, secret character of the Kingdom of God often totally surprises those who are impatient or who want immediate manifestations of power and glory.

When someone asks the question, "What has Christianity done for the world?" he has delivered himself into the hands of a "Kingdom presenter." The transforming power of Christianity is everywhere manifested. Many of the institutions we see today that manifest compassion and help to our broken world were begun by men and women on their knees.

The Kingdom, which includes the power of Christ and the purpose of God, is like a great river which for much of its course glides on beneath the ground unseen. But whenever it comes to the surface, its power and greatness is there for all to see it in action.

Perhaps it is incumbent upon us to ask personal questions that come to us from these parables. Does our personal witness maintain the pungency, the fire, and the activity manifested in the nature of the mustard seed? Can it be said of us, for instance, that there is in us the truth of the Gospel in an uncompromising presentation?

Let me push on even more personally. Are you aware of the influence of *things* in your life? Do you understand that materialism, loftiness, pride, and ambition can act like leaven in your life, causing you to compromise the nature of your witness?

You are probably familiar with the fact that Maundy Thursday begins the end of Holy Week. "Maundy" is a word for *mandatum* or *command*. On that night, Jesus said to His disciples, *"A new commandment I give to you, that you love one another; as I have loved you, that you also love one another"* (John 13:34). We must guard against any attitude that robs us of the opportunity for that kind of love and commitment.

Adding such leaven to the mixture in our lives will always complicate the way we use our gifts, talents, and abilities, which have been given to us in Christ. We become more concerned with personal ambition than in the purposes of the Kingdom. Loftiness and haughtiness are always distracting from the beauty and simplicity we are to be in Jesus!

Perhaps above all is the issue of impatience. These parables speak so eloquently to us on the nature of small beginnings. Are we content with such beginnings, whether corporate or personal? Can we hang around to wait for God to bring the results? Are we willing to do what God has called us to do, even when it means planting seeds that seem small and insignificant?

After all, everything does have a beginning. When God speaks a word, our part is to clear the ground; then it's time to watch the Father bring something out of nothing! The beginning often seems so insignificant. Are we willing to wait to let that beginning process of God begin? And are we willing to let eternity, *not* the present moment, determine the ultimate results?

Many years ago, Andre Crouch wrote these wonderful words:[87]

> To God be the glory....
> With His blood He has saved me,
> By His power He has raised me;
> To God be the glory
> For the things He has done.

The truth is, it *shall* be done!

Jesus prepares us to understand both the danger and the necessity of the Kingdom experience. History demands that we not be overwhelmed at any moment by what the Father is asking of us. The dynamic of transformation is always there; it is the dynamic of life. But we must always accept and walk it out one day at a time.

God grant us the courage to walk in obedience, living out our role in Christ's Kingdom in the era in which He has placed us. We share a wonderful privilege as part of the great ongoing river of Kingdom purpose!

# 18 TREASURE – WHO OR WHAT?

**P**eople love stories about lost treasure. The Indiana Jones films are just a sample of that interest, which is generated by the adventure, the risk, and, ultimately, the mystery and discovery that surround such pursuits.

Today's treasure hunter has gone high tech. Shovels and snorkels have been replaced by magnetometers and remote control vehicles, like the one used to discover and explore the Titanic. But the quarry hasn't changed. It's still the booty, the glint of gold — as well as a chance to shed fresh light on our past.

Mel Fisher is a real-life Indiana Jones. He found the shipwrecked Spanish galleon, the *Nuestra Senora de Atocha,* with four hundred million dollars in gold, silver, and emeralds. That search had taken him sixteen years of hunting, but on July 20, 1985, Mel Fisher at last found the remains of the ship that had sunk in 1622 during a hurricane off Key West at the southern tip of Florida.

The mother lode discovered on that afternoon in July was the biggest cache of sunken treasure ever found! In fact, you can actually see on display some of the gold, silver, and jewelry that was taken off the bottom of the ocean.

This find was actually an extraordinary climax to a seemingly impossible adventure. The sixty-two-year-old Mel Fisher had led an almost obsessive search for the wreckage of this Spanish galleon for years. He crisscrossed trails of artifacts scattered over miles of the ocean floor. He weathered personal tragedy and frequent bouts with near financial ruin. The actual discovery came ten years and one day after his oldest son and daughter-in-law had drowned pursuing this prize with which he was obsessed.

As we have seen, parables are metaphors or similes drawn from nature or common life that arrest the hearer's attention through their vividness or strangeness and often leave the mind in doubt about a precise application to one's life. This method of teaching is designed to tease the hearer into active thought, for parables are always heavenly truths wrapped in earthly stories.

## Truth Revealed or Concealed?

Let us now read parables five and six of Jesus' single discourse in Matthew 13. As is true with those we have already studied, these two parables also pertain to a specific subject — the Kingdom of God. Both are about a consummated search for treasure, about strategic wisdom, and about thoughtful, deliberate investment.

> "Again, the kingdom of heaven is like treasure hidden in a field, which a man found and hid; and for joy over it he goes and sells all that he has and buys that field.
> "Again, the kingdom of heaven is like a merchant seeking beautiful pearls,
> "who, when he had found one pearl of great price, went and sold all that he had and bought it."
>
> Matthew 13:44-46

Again, I believe it is important to remind ourselves that there is a multiple nature to parables. To those who are open-minded, humble, and inquisitive, parables give revelation. As Jesus said to His disciples, "... *To you it has been granted to know the mysteries of the*

*kingdom of heaven, but to them it has not been granted"* (Matt. 13:11
*NAS*). And again, Jesus continued:

> **"But blessed are your eyes, because they see; and your ears,
> because they hear.**
> **"For truly I say to you, that many prophets and righteous
> men desired to see what you see, and did not see it; and to hear
> what you hear, and did not hear it.**
>
> Matthew 13:16,17 NAS

So parables come with a revelational nature to those who are
humble as well as inquisitive about the nature of God's truth. But
we must remind ourselves that they also come as judgment on the
closed-minded — on those who are self-righteous and cynical about
life. That is why Jesus said earlier:

> **"For whoever has, to him more will be given, and he will
> have abundance; but whoever does not have, even what he has
> will be taken away from him.**
> **"Therefore I speak to them in parables, because seeing they
> do not see, and hearing they do not hear, nor do they under-
> stand.**
>
> Matthew 13:12,13

Jesus tells us here that parables can both *reveal* and *conceal* truth.
When the latter occurs, it confirms people in their sin and rebellion.

A case in point is what happened after Jesus taught His listeners
using the parable of the vine grower. The religious leaders who were
there sought to seize Jesus and kill Him right after that teaching
(Mark 12:12), for they often came to listen only to judge and thus
confirm their rebellion against God. They did not want to change!

A very positive result of parables is given to us in the Old
Testament. In Second Samuel 12, we are told that a friend of King
David, a prophet, came to him one day with a parable. The purpose
of that parable was to show David that nothing was hidden from
God's sight. It also revealed that David had committed murder
following an act of adultery. Through that parable, judgment came

into David's life. As a result, he repented and received God's judgment and then went on to fulfill the purpose of God for his life.

We can see from this account that parables are persuasive. They are meant to become a turning point for our lives. They are designed to convince us to give everything for Jesus Christ — to turn over our entire lives to Him.

## The Purpose of Studying The Kingdom of God

Now back to our study in Matthew 13. The great theme of Jesus' teaching here was *the Kingdom of God*. However, we could actually summarize everything Jesus did and taught during His earthly ministry with that same phrase. Certainly it was Jesus' primary topic during the Sermon on the Mount, as He taught the people, "When you pray, pray, 'Thy kingdom come, thy will be done'" and "Seek first the Kingdom of God" (Matt. 6:7-10, 33).

The common thread that tied this theme together throughout Jesus' ministry was His message to the people to "repent." Why was this the message He proclaimed wherever He went? Because, as Jesus was careful to explain, "The Kingdom of God is at hand" (Matt. 4:17) and "You must be born again to enter the Kingdom" (John 3:3).

The nature of the Kingdom of God was indeed the key and the major thrust of Jesus' instruction to His disciples. This issue was also a major source of controversy between Jesus and the Jewish leaders; in fact, it became the ultimate determining factor at Jesus' trial. Jesus was questioned regarding His Kingdom and proclaimed Himself a King. In the end, it was for this that He was crucified (*see* John 18:36,37).

Finally, we must also see that the Kingdom of God was the message of Jesus' post-resurrection ministry. The Word declares that for forty days after His resurrection and before His ascension, Jesus taught His disciples about the Kingdom of God (Acts 1:3).

Do you see how important it is to understand this teaching? *We need to grasp what the Bible teaches us about the Kingdom of God.*

Several definitions have been given of the Kingdom of God in this discussion. Most simply, it is a phrase that refers to the sovereign rule and reign of the glorious King Himself! Therefore, these parables we are studying demonstrate:

- How God's Kingdom operates in the various spheres of life on this earth.
- How God's rule and His will intersect with our lives.
- How we enter into that Kingdom and come under the Lordship of Jesus Christ.

Thus, when Jesus teaches parables, it is meant to bring us under the rule of God and the lordship of Jesus Christ in order to bring about His purpose in our lives.

## Who Is the Treasure, Who Is the Man?

In these next two parables, Jesus first compares the Kingdom of Heaven to hidden treasure in a field. When a man discovers the treasure, he hides it until he can sell everything he owns in order to buy the entire field. The listeners would have understood this parable, for Jewish civil law accorded to anyone buying a field all that was in the field. Thus, the man who found the treasure hid it in order to keep it from being discovered by thieves or even by the current property owner.

So also Jesus compares the Kingdom of God to a merchant seeking fine pearls. When the merchant finds the "pearl of great price," he, too, sells everything he has to obtain the treasure he has discovered.

Now, remember that Jesus is telling this parable, as well as the next two parables, to the disciples *alone*. No interpretation from the

Master is recorded, and as two thousand years of Christian commentary have proven, these two parables can indeed seem mysterious.

The first problem in the treasure parable is this: *Who* or *what* is represented by "the treasure"? The second problem is *who* is the man who finds it, hides it again, sells everything he has, and buys the whole field — all for the joy of it?

Some say it is Jesus who finds the treasure and then sells everything He has to buy the treasure. In this interpretation or teaching, the treasure represents Israel, God's unique possession. However, Jesus didn't come upon Israel by accident. His coming to them was foretold and planned. Nor did He rejoice over the people of Israel, since ultimately they rejected Him. In fact, Jesus mourned over them!

Needless to say, we could spend a great deal of time comparing theory to theory. I refer you to what I believe is one of the most original discussions on this passage in Robert Farrar Capon's enlightening and well-written book called *The Parables of Grace*. I urge you to accept the challenge to read that book and become more informed on these two parables of Jesus. Meanwhile, this smaller book has a more specific challenge: to see how each parable in Matthew 13 flows consistently and consecutively within a single discourse of Jesus on the *continuing nature* of the Kingdom of God, from His resurrection to the day He comes again.

Every preceding parable has emphasized the value of human beings who embody Kingdom principle in their lives and thus influence the age in which they live. It might even be said that the ultimate mystery of the Kingdom is the way God chooses, scatters, and prospers the planting of individuals, entrusting His work to mere humans who, empowered by His Holy Spirit, carry out His divine purpose.

That fact matters greatly as we interpret these two parables. They lie in an already prepared field of truth. We cannot lift these two from the thread of the single-discourse discussion.

Now, traditionally most evangelicals have given these two parables a simple but *man-centered* interpretation. The treasure or the pearl represents either eternal life, Christ, or salvation. The man and the merchant in both these parables represents the sinner. The sinner is pursuing Christ, so he pays all to receive Jesus and to gain salvation.

But if we interpret these parables this way, we risk the dangerous conclusion that salvation is purchased by the sinner. I submit that this is simply the wrong way to look at what Jesus is teaching here. As one recent writer concludes:

> To make the treasure in the field mean salvation, would make the man who bought it the sinner and would violate the scriptural picture of the unregenerate. No sinner looks upon the hidden treasure of salvation with joy; he does not even know that it is there hidden in the field. He would not sacrifice all that he had in order to buy it. In addition to all this, it is not for sale at any price. Such an interpretation is the essence of legalism, Pelagianism, Arminianism, and the modern concept of salvation on the basis of human merit.[88]

I believe the Christ-centered interpretation of these twin parables of discovery is entirely different. The field in which the treasure is hidden and the sea in which the pearl was cultured or formed in the oyster both represent the world or the age we live in. Both the man and the merchant are Jesus, the Son of Man. The treasure and the pearl both represent mankind, or the masses of unevangelized humanity.

## Jesus, Our 'Indiana Jones'

Here, then, must begin the ground-zero interpretation of this parable. If we apprehend and grasp what the parable is teaching us, it will radically revolutionize our approach to ourselves, to others, and to this world in general!

Jesus, as it were, is the "Indiana Jones" of this parable, pursuing us at all costs. The difference is that He already knows everything about us; yet still He pursues and seeks. Meditate on that for a moment. According to Luke 19:10, we are being pursued by the Spirit of Jesus, sent by the Father to find us: *"For the Son of Man has come to seek and to save that which was lost."*

A recent convert once rose in a meeting to give his testimony to God's saving grace. He told how the Lord had won his heart and delivered him from the guilt and power of sin. He spoke freely of Christ and His work, but said nothing of his own efforts.

The leader of the meeting was of a legalistic background. So when the man was finished giving his testimony, the leader said, "Our dear brother has told us of the Lord's part in his salvation. But when I was converted, there was a whole lot *I had to do myself* before I could expect the Lord to do anything for me. Brother, didn't you do your part first before God did His part to save you?"

The man was on his feet in an instant. He replied, "Yes, Sir, I clearly forgot. I didn't tell you about my part, did I? Well, I did my part for over thirty years, running away from God as fast as my sins would carry me. *That was my part!* But God was after me until He ran me down. That was *His* part!"

When God called the people of Israel, He said to them, "I found you like a treasure. I treasured you among all the peoples of the earth" (Exod. 19:5). Now Jesus is talking about finding and then hiding a treasure; going first to sell all He has in order to buy the whole field. He speaks, I believe, of how He came to the Jews, only to have them reject His ministry as Messiah.

But, of course, Jesus will come to Israel again. He paid the full price and He will come again to find them, His treasure among the nations. That is yet to happen.

## The Treasure vs. the Pearl

The pearl in the second parable is more likely to speak of the Gentiles, because to a Jew (and Matthew is writing to Jewish Christians), a pearl didn't hold the same value as did gold, silver, or emeralds. This is evident when studying one of the garments of the high priest, who served on behalf of the people of Israel before God. The high priest wore a breastplate with the names of the twelve tribes of Israel. The stones on that breastplate were all semi-precious stones; not one was a pearl.

On the other hand, the Gentiles would relate more to Jesus' parable of the pearl than they would to that of the treasure, for the pearl held great value to them. Thus in the second parable, Jesus was speaking of the Church He would win for Himself. Out of the "oyster shell" masses of humanity, He would find the Church, His pearl of great price. And of His own volition, He would lay down His life to purchase that pearl as His own.

## Our Message to the World: 'God Is Pursuing You!'

But where does this interpretation place us today? How should our message, our mission, and our methods as individuals and as the Church reflect the Kingdom of God as revealed in Jesus Christ? For one thing, these parables should determine what our unique stories are of how we came to the Lord. Our focus should be on *telling who Jesus Christ is*, for this will determine the scope of our audience.

Perhaps the first thing we need to say to each other and to the world, is this: "You are being pursued in love by God." Try *that* on someone and see what happens! Recently I did that. I said to someone, "I'm not pursuing you. I'm just agreeing with the fact that *God* is pursuing you in Jesus Christ and that He loves you." I discovered that approach wakes up people real quickly!

The world thinks that *they* are pursuing *God*. People try to do something to get His attention, crying out, "Help me down here,

Lord! You know I'm in a crisis. Help me!" But in truth, God is saying, "I am pursuing *you*. I see just where you're at, and I'm after you!"

## Buy the Whole Field!

The man who discovered the treasure didn't simply buy a cubic yard or so of nice, clean dirt in which to cleverly bury it. "He bought the whole property: sinkholes, dung heaps, poison ivy, and sticker bushes, plus all the rats, mice, flies, and beetles that came with it."[89]

So, too, should the Church respond to the "people treasures" lying hidden in the field of the world. If the Church can't bring itself to buy all kinds and conditions of human beings — white and non-white, male and female, smart and stupid, good and bad, spiritual and non-spiritual — it can't even begin to pretend that it is catholic in its outreach.

We must be willing to buy the whole field to get the treasure! We can't just slice up society like a pie and separate those we want to pursue in the name of Christ from those we do not wish to pursue. To be faithful to the message of the Kingdom, we have to recognize that God pursued and bought *all* in Jesus Christ. Then we need to break down our homogenized approach to Christianity, eliminating our prejudices and racist attitudes that have erected so many social and economic barriers.

In the name of Jesus and for the sake of the Kingdom of God, we must draw a circle much bigger than we have been willing to draw in the past. The Kingdom of God will include many more than we can conceive. We really don't have a choice in the matter.

# 19

# PEARLS IN ODD PLACES

J oseph Conrad, the world-famous writer, once said, "There is no getting away from a treasure that once fastens upon your mind."[90] Someone else remarked that *our values determine our distance.* How far will we go and how much we will pay always depends on how much we value an object. In Jesus' day, the search for pearls would drive a merchant to travel throughout the entire Middle Eastern world and even as far as India.

Thus, Jesus' parable of the pearl presented a familiar story: *"Again, the kingdom of heaven is like a merchant seeking beautiful pearls, who, when he had found one pearl of great price, went and sold all that he had and bought it"* (Matt. 13:46,47).

Christian literature abounds with messages and teachings on this "pearl of great price," for it is a magnificent image. The merchant said, "This is like nothing else I've ever seen!" and was therefore willing to sell all he had to buy the prize. Can you imagine such a find — a pearl that is worth everything you've accumulated in your entire lifetime?

In the last chapter, we talked about Mel Fisher's search for the Spanish ship, the *Nuestra Senora de Atocha.* Four years into Fisher's search, his team found the ship anchor and three bars of silver. However, Fisher had spent a great deal of time researching Spanish galleons. During his research, he had discovered that the *Atocha* had been laden with gold as it returned from the West Indies in order to help the king of Spain pay off his national debts. Fisher knew there had to be more to find than an anchor and a few bars of silver, so he continued to pursue his vision for the next twelve years and, like the pearl merchant, at great personal sacrifice.

Again and again, Fisher crisscrossed the area of the Florida Keys, searching for the coveted treasure ship. Twelve years later, he finally found the mother lode more than seven miles away from his earlier, partial find. Indeed, what people see and what they hope for are the things that give them the energy to keep going!

## The Pearl of Great Price — The Church

We must remind ourselves that in this parable, "the Kingdom of God" is like the merchant who is seeking for beautiful pearls and who ultimately sells everything to purchase one pearl of great price.

Jesus is indeed a Person of infinite beauty, and to know Him is worth any price. Yet we have seen that this pearl of great worth cannot represent salvation through Christ, for although salvation is won at great sacrifice, it cannot be sought or bought by human effort. I must believe, on the basis of everything we've seen in our prior discussions, that this great pearl *does* indeed represent the Church, valued and known by God before the casting down of the earth's foundations.

In Ephesians 1:18, Paul described this "pearl of great price" as *"...the riches of the glory of His inheritance in the saints."* Indeed, this was the mystery:

> **That the Gentiles should be fellow heirs, of the same body, and partakers of His promise in Christ through the gospel....**

> To the intent that now the manifold wisdom of God might
> be made known by the church to the principalities and powers
> in the heavenly places.
>
> Ephesians 3:6,10

There is no more touching scripture to me than Second Corinthians 8:9: *"For you know the grace of our Lord Jesus Christ, that though He was rich, yet for your sakes He became poor, that you through His poverty might become rich."* Indeed, I believe both of these parables underscore the price Jesus paid on the Cross to purchase the field for its treasure and that one pearl of great price. When the Father looked at planet earth, He saw a treasure of such great worth that He was willing to give His best, His only Son, to purchase the prize.

## Seeing People as *Treasure*

But to be consistent with the order of these seven parables, we must add that there is a message here *for* us and not simply *about* us — the message that proclaims the incredible value and potential of the people of this earth. All of mankind is a treasure of inestimable worth in the eyes of God, and we dare not see people as any less than this in *our* view! Again, Capon leads us to an imperative understanding:

> The church, like the purchaser of the field, can never afford to leave "unbought" any part of the earthly field in which God has hidden the treasure of the mystery. It does not dare to risk its own sure knowledge of where the mystery of the Word is — to risk its certainty that it has the right name of the Word (Jesus) and that it knows the precise location (the Incarnation) of the treasure that makes the world precious — by failing to purchase to itself every last bit of the field.[91]

This is a message the world must hear. Each person has been created in the image of God, and although that likeness has been distorted by sin, he or she nevertheless represents an irreplaceable treasure to the Creator.

In the deepest sense, we as Kingdom sons and daughters must see the people of this world as *treasure* — *not* as a problem. God saw this treasure on the earth and sold all to buy it. For us, it may be our neighbor or employer for whom we must be willing to sell all to purchase that person's value for the Kingdom of God. The field in a sense is the price we must pay, but people are always the treasure.

This doesn't mean we must remain unaware of the racial, political, and sexual problems of our age. True intercession proceeds from identification. We are to stand against self-righteous judgment as we stand on behalf of those without hope.

Isaiah 53:12 declares that Jesus was *"...numbered with the transgressors, and He bore the sin of many, and made intercession for the transgressors."* The word "numbered" here basically means *identified with*, as though Jesus has said, "When you try to divide humanity into groups and categories, you must count Me with the transgressors. I identify *with* them that I might intercede *for* them." In actual fact, the religious leaders did count Jesus as a friend of winebibbers, prostitutes, and sinners.

People are the Lord's crowns, and He claims sovereign rights over the people of the world even before they are truly responsive to His Kingdom authority. It is clear from Psalm 2, the great Messianic psalm, that the nations are the Lord's inheritance: *"Ask of Me, and I will give You the nations for Your inheritance, and the ends of the earth for Your possession"* (v. 8).[92]

Let's be honest. The teaching of the Kingdom of God challenges our idea of mission. It demands that we look at people in a different manner. *What we see in our neighbors, our fellow workers, our spouse, or a desperate person on the street will determine the price we will pay and how far we will go to help them determine their true value.*

If all I see in people's lives are the destructive patterns and external rebelliousness, I will have little to do with them. It is, after all, what we see and what we hope for that gives us the energy to keep pursuing people after initial rejections.

*"Looking unto Jesus,"* writes the author of Hebrews, *"the author and finisher of our faith, who for the joy that was set before Him endured the cross, despising the shame, and has sat down at the right hand of the throne of God"* (Heb. 12:2). This was the same discoverer of the treasure in the field who *"...for joy over it he goes and sells all that he has and buys that field"* (Matt. 13:44). Similarly, the pearl merchant, *"...when he had found one pearl of great price, went and sold all that he had and bought it"* (v. 46). In just such a way, our intensity of desire to seek out the treasure will feed *our* effectiveness in the Kingdom of God.

## We Need the Treasure
## In the Field

The following words should greatly challenge us:

How many opportunities to proclaim the mystery has the church missed, because it never took the time to learn the "language," cultural or historical, spiritual, or practical, of the people it addressed? How often have the "unchurched," the great catholic mass [*note:* this author is not talking about the Catholic church, but about the universal mass of people] of unevangelized humanity who are, mind you, the very field in which the treasure of Jesus is already hidden, and who, but for their unbelief, would be enjoying Him as mightily as believers do — how often have the unchurched put up a "not for sale" sign on their farm, because they simply couldn't stand the arrogance of Christians?[93]

For many years of Bible study, I have been fascinated by a story in First Samuel 30. Its context is David's strife with the Amalekites, especially after they attacked his headquarters village at Ziklag, burning it with fire and taking captive the women and children who had been left there. When David and his men returned to this destruction, they were so sorrowful that the men even spoke of stoning David himself!

But God instructed David to take his men and pursue the Amalekites. On their way, they encountered a young Egyptian slave. Let the rest of the story tell itself.

> Then they found an Egyptian in the field, and brought him to David; and they gave him bread and he ate, and they let him drink water.
>
> And they gave him a piece of a cake of figs and two clusters of raisins. So when he had eaten, his strength came back to him; for he had eaten no bread nor drunk water for three days and three nights.
>
> Then David said to him, "To whom do you belong, and where are you from?" And he said, "I am a young man from Egypt, servant of an Amalekite; and my master left me behind, because three days ago I fell sick.
>
> "We made an invasion of the southern area of the Cherethites, in the territory which belongs to Judah, and of the southern area of Caleb; and we burned Ziklag with fire."
>
> And David said to him, "Can you take me down to this troop?" And he said, "Swear to me by God that you will neither kill me nor deliver me into the hands of my master, and I will take you down to this troop."

1 Samuel 30:11-15

The rest, as they say, is history. David attacked and won a great victory, rescuing all their wives, sons, and daughters and recovering all that had been taken from him and his men. The simple truth of the matter is this: *The Egyptian boy, whom David rescued and treated both kindly and generously, became the key to David's victory.*

We need the treasure in the field, for the prostitute, drug dealer, and street person know where the enemy is. It thus must be understood that without them, we're lost, and without us, they're dead!

Recently a newspaper ran a story about a man who had gone to the store to purchase market-value oysters for some bouillabaisse he was making at home. Imagine his amazement and surprise when he opened an oyster and discovered one of the largest black pearls in history! It was a pearl of such great value that no immediate price could be placed on it.

Kingdom work is often a series of such amazing discoveries. We can never know in truth the ultimate results of our compassion, our acceptance, and our witness.

# 20 BUY OFF THE WRONG INFLUENCES

You may already know that a pearl is a response to an injury. Sand or some other irritant gets into the oyster shell and causes the oyster to secrete a substance we call "mother of pearl." Over time, the soft inner membrane of the oyster becomes a formed pearl. The size and quality of that pearl are often directly proportional to the injury suffered and the response given!

We must be reminded personally of our own worth to the Lord and the Kingdom of God. None of us is in fact incidental, nor should we ever see our circumstances, however different, as happenstance. Not one of us is an accident. God placed an infinite value on us from the foundation of the world and therefore paid an infinite price for our redemption.

Sometimes we must look into the face of Christ. As we look into His eyes, we will discover a treasure beyond belief — the reflection of who we are in His eyes. Indeed, we are pearls of great value and have only increased in size and value as a result of the difficulties we have encountered in life.

## Pay the Price for Your Potential

Perhaps this short chapter seems parenthetical and, I admit, unattached to the rest. But I believe it is imperative to our ultimate purpose. As the Father God looks at each of us individually, He sees within us this infinite treasure — a "good deal," a pearl worth an infinite price. This treasure lies hidden within us, as it were, in the field of our lives. And even though there is a mixing of metaphors, Jesus' message remains the same: We must be willing to pay a price for the productivity and potential in our lives.

A fellow teacher, Charlie Elwell, who has pastored many years in the state of New York, explains this truth in an amazingly revealing personal story. Charlie grew up in a poor and simple family. His father owned a very small farm with even less arable land. All the family worked hard to maximize each crop. It was truly subsistence farming.

Across a broken fence was an overgrown and seemingly abandoned property, but Charlie's father was convinced by the lay of the land that it was wonderful soil. One day he ventured into the old farm with Charlie and dug up a small shovelful of land. The soil was amazingly rich and black and would obviously produce marvelous crops.

So Charlie's dad investigated the county records and obtained the name of the registered owner. In the months that followed, he took many trips to see the owner, presenting a new offer each time to rent or lease the abandoned fields. In each negotiation, an agreement would at first seem possible but would then fall through. In desperation, Charlie's father offered to give the owner a substantial profit on the land, even offering to rent the soil for only one day a week!

Finally, Charlie's father wearied the older farmer. "You see," the owner finally admitted, "I want to rent or even to sell this land to you, but I don't really own it." He then described his situation: More than thirteen old cousins — very distant relatives — would have to be located and convinced to sign off on the contract individually. It proved to be an impossible task. It was a valuable farm, a treasure in waiting, but a bunch of unconcerned old men succeeded in tying up the value of the farm, thus preventing it from fulfilling its purpose.

Now consider a similar situation that occurs every day in the lives of believers. Paul writes in First Corinthians 3:9: "...*You are God's field....*" Or as J. B. Phillips translates it, "...*You are a field under God's cultivation....*"[94]

The context of this word "field" is a discussion of what will happen to some believers at the Judgment Seat of Christ. These believers are built on the foundation of Jesus Christ and belong to God, but they will "suffer loss" as they watch all they have built in life by their own efforts burned by the testing fire, although they themselves "...*will be saved, yet so as through fire*" (1 Cor. 3:15). In other words, these "fallow fields" that never fulfilled their God-ordained purpose will make it into Heaven "by the skin of their teeth"!

## Get Rid of the 'Old Cousins'!

How can a valuable "treasure-field" become useless, a place for brambles and thorns? How can the garden spot of our lives become overgrown and nonproductive? Probably because there are too many "old cousins" in our lives! As Paul writes, *Knowing this, that our old man* [the man of old] *was crucified with Him, that the body of sin might be done away with, that WE SHOULD no longer be slaves of sin*" (Rom. 6:6).

But Paul makes it clear what we must do:

> ...Reckon yourselves to be dead indeed to sin, but alive to God in Christ Jesus our Lord.
> Therefore do not let sin reign in your mortal body, that you should obey it in its lusts.
>
> **Romans 6:11,12**

There is such a difference between what is true spiritually — the victory has been paid for, the property redeemed — and the nagging reality of our daily, practical, worldly lives. Do you see the reason for this last look at the parables of the treasure in the field and the pearl of great price? We also must sell all to buy or release the full potential in our lives. Indeed, whatever territory of our lives we give over to Satan, he takes and begins to rule like a maharajah!

Thus, we see that the Word is always personal to us. It demands our decision and discipleship.

> **And do not present your members as instruments of unrighteousness to sin, but present yourselves to God as being alive from the dead, and your members as instruments of righteousness to God.**
> **For sin shall not have dominion over you, for you are not under law but under grace.**
>
> **Romans 6:13,14**

Kingdom of God economy is never automatic. There is a price we must pay, a treasure and value we must personally release. I don't need these distant relatives exercising a negative influence in my life. One by one I must make sure that every non-Christ authority "signs off," willingly or by force, from exercising any influence over me. I have been bought with a price, and I intend to glorify God with my life!

# 21 JESUS' FINALE – THE NET

With these final chapters, we finish this devotional yet reverent view of Jesus' one specific discourse on the Kingdom of God. Inspired authors didn't determine what to include or in what order to set this particular teaching. The Son of Man Himself determined the subject, the order, and, when necessary, the commentary and explanation. Matthew 13 is unusually holy ground, and the student should approach its material with an underlined sense of holiness and care.

The finale of Jesus' actual message is the very verse that establishes the set nature of His teaching: *"Now it came to pass, when Jesus had finished these parables, that he departed from there"* (v. 53). Thus, we see that our Master taught these parables all on one occasion and in this specific order.

It is interesting to note, however, that the writer of this Gospel seems to couple this set discourse with Jesus' rejection at the synagogue in Nazareth (vv. 54-58). Although this last paragraph is unattached to Jesus' teaching on the Kingdom, it nevertheless seems hauntingly applicable and necessary.[95]

## Creating the Right
## Atmosphere for Truth

After Jesus departed from the seaside, He journeyed to His hometown and was found teaching in His boyhood synagogue. Those who attended the service were astonished as they listened to Him. However, they weren't reacting to the quality of Jesus' teaching; rather, they were insulted that the Person who was teaching with such wisdom shared common roots with them!

The people asked, *"...Where did this Man get this wisdom and these mighty works?"* (v. 54). This was a seemingly appropriate question; however, the next statement from their mouths assures us that theirs was not an honest search for knowledge:

> "Is this not the carpenter's son? Is not His mother called Mary? And His brothers James, Joses, Simon, and Judas?
> "And His sisters, are they not all with us? Where then did this Man get all these things?"

> Matthew 13:55,56

The people in Jesus' hometown of Nazareth were prejudiced and critical and therefore unable to receive. They were making a judgment according to *background* and *family connections* rather than according to *who Jesus was*. Since none of Jesus' brothers believed during His lifetime, this judgment may well have included an attitude of "He's not even effective with his own family!"

William Barclay writes, "Many a message has been killed stone dead, not because there was anything wrong with the message, but because the minds of the people were so prejudiced against the messenger that the message never had a chance."[96]

This kind of judgment is too often the case today in the church, in academia, and in publishing. An overly critical atmosphere is often a barrier through which no word can penetrate. Indeed, the listener or, in this case, the reader carries more than half the responsibility for results. A congregation preaches more than half the sermon; a reader creates much of the atmosphere for his acceptance or rejection of truth. Yet how wonderfully this principle can work to a person's benefit! There can be such an expectancy, such an eagerness to hear the Holy Spirit, that even the poorest sermon or book becomes a living flame.

When Jesus spoke in Nazareth, He was met with "hostility and incredulity." The people couldn't conceive that anyone who had been raised among them and who lacked the necessary credentials — someone whose father and mother, sisters and brothers had lived among them all their lives — could actually be the long-awaited Messiah whom the prophets had foretold. As William Barclay said, "The prophet, as so often happens, had no honour in his own country; and their attitude to Him raised a barrier which made it impossible for Jesus to have any effect upon them."[97]

As a result, the people *"...were offended* [scandalized] *at Him.... Now He did not do many mighty works there because of their unbelief"* (Matt. 13:57,58). Luke later records a similar thought in Jesus' words concerning Jerusalem (and Israel in general): *"...You did not know the time of your visitation"* (Luke 19:44). The word "visitation" here carries the meaning of *oversight* or *gracious superintendence.*

It is so often our level of expectancy that either advances our understanding or crushes our opportunity. Therefore, I would challenge you to study the word *offense* in the Scriptures, for time and time again, this is the ultimate cause of our bondage and darkness. Indeed, as the proverb states, *"A brother offended is harder to win than a strong city..."* (Prov. 18:19).

## The 'Wrap-up': The Parable of the Dragnet

"Enough!" you might say. "Get back to the subject." And so we will. But this final paragraph that Matthew included may very well "set the table" for our discussion of Jesus' final and most controversial parable in this particular discourse. Although often referred to as "the parable of the net," it is, as we shall see, much more specific than that. Herein lies the difficulty, since Jesus begins by saying, "...*The kingdom of heaven is like a dragnet that was cast into the sea...*" (Matt. 13:47).

As we have seen, a parable is a comparison that puts one thing beside another to make a point. If we run from the *comparison*, we will completely miss the point! We must also remind ourselves that the honest and sincere person catches the meaning of Jesus' stories, whereas the merely curious or critical generally miss the point entirely.[98]

The parable of the dragnet is unique to the Gospel of Matthew, as is the parable of the wheat and the tares. Further, the specific verb tense in this parable makes it clear that it is *not* about the ultimate, consummated, or finished Kingdom ("the not yet" Kingdom); otherwise, Jesus would have spoken in the future tense. Neither is it about the beginning of the Kingdom, because in that case, He would have used the present tense.

Clearly this parable is about the Kingdom as it has become. In other words, it is about the situation that now exists in the "latter days" following the Cross — the Kingdom during God's final dealings with the world. (Please keep in mind that the Kingdom is greater than the Church, although the Church is a living type and sacrament of the Kingdom.)

This final parable of Jesus' sermon is a wrap-up indeed. You see, like an airplane flight, there are two points of time in a sermon that are the most dangerous: the beginning and the ending. Good speakers always have a fitting climax to their sermons, and Jesus clearly chose this parable to be the end of His discourse on the Kingdom of God, or the Kingdom of Heaven. And what a grand finale He chose: the wrap-up of the final age (although not the end of the cosmos) and of God's dealings with mankind through the Cross.

Let us begin, as we should, with Jesus' teaching:

"Again, the kingdom of heaven is like a dragnet that was cast into the sea and gathered some of every kind,

"which, when it was full, they drew to shore; and they sat down and gathered the good into vessels, but threw the bad away.

"So it will be at the end of the age. The angels will come forth, separate the wicked from among the just,

"and cast them into the furnace of fire. There will be wailing and gnashing of teeth."

Matthew 13:47-50

You will note that as in the parable of the wheat and the tares, Jesus again speaks openly and clearly of the end and the destruction of evil. He is also specific about the pitiful nature of eternal judgment, where people are cast *"...into the furnace of fire. There will be wailing and gnashing of teeth"* (v. 50).

So in two of these seven parables, Jesus deals clearly with a specific end of this age. However, from the Cross to this present moment, this age is pregnant with opportunity for people to be saved and to come to know God, reconciled to Him through the provision and peace found in a personal faith and confession of Jesus Christ as Savior and Lord.

## Live With an Understanding Of the End of the Age

Clearly, we must all live with a wise understanding of the end of our days, whether we are sixteen or sixty-four years old. For more than a year at the end of His ministry, Jesus spoke of His coming death and the end of His earthly ministry. But He wasn't being morbid. In fact, one of Jesus' best jokes was in reference to the Pharisees' warning concerning Herod: *"...Get out and depart from here, for Herod wants to kill You"* (Luke 13:31). (I wonder how they knew that!)

Jesus replied to them, *"...Go tell that fox* [the actual word was probably "jackal"], *'Behold, I cast out demons and perform cures today and tomorrow, and the third day I shall be perfected'"* (Luke 13:32). Jesus was saying in essence, "Here I am, and here I will be, doing the will of My Father. I will finish My work before My life is finished." Jesus spoke again of the events that would soon transpire in another setting, saying, *"You know that after two days is the Passover, and the Son of Man will be delivered up to be crucified"* (Matt. 26:2).

I can't emphasize this too much: We must never be too fascinated with this present age! It's as passing as a sand castle before the tide comes in. We should never build our hopes on such a tenuous foundation. A tidal wave is coming that will sweep away the sand castles of this present era.

With a keen understanding of their own limited time on this earth, my beloved parents kept a plaster plaque on the dining room wall that read:

**Only one life, 'twill soon be past.**
**Only what's done for Christ will last.**

My parents grasped the truth set forth by the writer to the Hebrews: *"And as it is appointed for men to die once, but after this the judgment"* (Heb. 9:27). We would do well to stay ever aware of this truth as well, for no one escapes death's appointment, and no age will survive forever.

# 22
# SEINE MEN AND WOMEN OF THE KINGDOM

J ust what is this net to which Jesus compares the Kingdom of God in its ministry within this current age? Specifically, it is a type of net not used any other place in the New Testament. Today such a net is called a *seine*; here it is called by its Greek name *sagene*. (The word "seine" is actually derived through Latin or French from this Greek word *sagene*.)

We must note here that two other words are also used for "net" in the Greek text: a throw net (used twice), and the general word for net, which is used twelve times in the New Testament. Each of these nets performs a specific function that is described by its name.

The *sagene*, used only this once in the New Testament, is itself a net with a particular kind of function. This net is normally dragged through the water, taking in everything in its path without discrimination. As we move through this chapter, we will spend some time discussing this type of net in order to thoroughly underline Jesus' comparison between the net and the Kingdom of God. But you must know from the outset that even today, the seine net scoops up in its gathering movement "some of every kind" (v. 47) — boots, glass, seaweed, fish of every sort, beer bottles, marine debris, and a wide variety of creeping things.

Robert Farrar Capon, an unusually provocative writer to whom I am often indebted, writes the following:

> "But *sagene*, appearing as it does only in this passage, is a particular kind of net, namely, one that is dragged through the water, indiscriminately taking in everything in its path. Accordingly, the kingdom of heaven (and by extension, the church as the sacrament of that kingdom) manifests the same indiscriminateness. [99]

## The Use of a Seine
## In Biblical Days

The dragnet or seine is said to be the oldest type of fishing net, and its use was once the most important fishing method on the Sea of Galilee. In the Hebrew Scriptures and in the Talmud, this net is called a *herem*. Egyptian tomb paintings that date from the third millennium BC suggest the wide acceptance and use of such nets throughout Eastern nations in ancient times.

In fact, the dragnet (although used only once in the New Testament) is used nine times in the Hebrew Scriptures. Ezekiel, for example, references this net three times when talking about a "place to spread seines" (26:5,14; 47:10). The drying of these huge nets was a constant and familiar sight in fishing villages. The Jerusalem Talmud calls the fishermen of Tiberias *ha-raMEte-ver-YAH* or "the seine men of Tiberias."[100]

This seining was no easy process. The average net was approximately 250 meters (820 feet) long. It was nine feet at its wings and twenty-six feet at its center. The bottom row of the net was weighted with sinkers and the head had cork floats. As many as sixteen men were required to haul the catch into shore using lines attached to each end. Mendel Nun writes:

> Once the hauling begins, the motion must be continuous. As long as the net is advancing, the fish face the net trying to escape rather than swimming away from it. However,

if the pulling motion were even briefly stopped before the net reached the shore, the fish would escape.[101]

He continues with an interesting scripture from the Old Testament:

> In Habakkuk 1:14-15 we find a reference to seine fishing that is generally translated inaccurately. Correctly translated the passage should read: "You have made the righteous like fish in the sea, like sea creatures that have no ruler. He [the evildoer] has caught them all with a hook, hauled them up in his seine, gathered them in his trapnet. That is why he rejoices and is glad."[102]

## Gathering 'Some of Every Kind'

Several writers have called attention to the fact that there is no mention of fish in this dragnet comparison to the Kingdom. Jesus' attention is on how the Kingdom works in this era, gathering *some of every kind* from the vast variety within the sea of humanity.

Interestingly, John 12:32 is almost always translated, *"And I, if I be lifted up from the earth, will draw all MEN to Myself"* (NAS). Occasionally the phrase is translated "draw all *peoples*," but in every case the word is italicized, which means it is not in the original manuscripts. In other words, Jesus actually said, *"I will draw ALL to Myself"* — exactly as this dragnet does in this parable!

Clearly our expectation regarding the Kingdom of God in this age must be that it is *inclusive* and never *exclusive* in nature. The following quote from Capon, although quite long, contains certain truths that are imperative to our understanding of this issue.

> Which leads to a second reflection: If the kingdom works like a dragnet, gathering every kind, *the church, as the sacrament of the kingdom, should avoid the temptation to act like a sport fisherman* who is interested only in speckled trout and hand-tied flies. In particular, *it should not get itself into*

*the habit of rejecting as junk the flotsam and jetsam of the world* — the human counterparts of the old boots, bottles, and beer cans that a truly catholic fishing operation will inevitably dredge up. Because while the kingdom itself will indeed make it onto the eschatological beach, the church, as now operative, will not. The church is only the sacrament of the kingdom — a visible sign of a presently invisible mystery. But in the Last Day, the church as such will not be necessary at all; the mystery of the kingdom will stand revealed in and of itself and will need no sacraments or signs whatsoever.[103]

## What Is Our Response To the 'Bad Ones'?

My third grandson, Wesley Clinton Langskov, was born in the lower bedroom of our home. There had been more than a little hope and a seeming confirmation that he would be a girl. You know how prospective mothers can be sometimes, saying, "I'm carrying this one different," and so forth. Even the midwife had suggested the eventuality of a baby girl.

But when my lovely daughter went into labor, God spoke clearly to me that this baby would grow to become a man of faith and power. Now, I'm not given to many specific "words" from the Lord — let alone *those* words! But my grandson Wes has lived up to that prophetic word. He is an unusually consecrated and a remarkable young man.

For several years, I had an older mobile home parked on a California lake reservoir near my pastorate. It was a very special retreat and a wonderful place to work and study. My son-in-law Jeff (Wesley's dad) taught all his sons to fish on that lake. I have several pictures of him standing on the pier with all four sons alongside, each with their pole in the water. What a beautiful image!

On one such day, Wes turned to Jeff and said, "Dad, I want to catch a catfish!" Before Jeff could answer, an older experienced fisherman called out, "Son, this is a lagoon that often dries out during the summer. There are no catfish here — you have to go out on the main body of the lake."

Unexpectedly, Wes began to cry, so his dad said, "Well, just pray about it, Wes!" I have no idea what this lad prayed, but it must have been powerful. Within five minutes, he was pulling in the biggest, ugliest catfish that folks up there had seen in some time. In fact, the whiskered, pug-nosed, dirty gray fish so scared Wes when it surfaced that he dropped the pole and ran down the pier!

Coincidentally, the "bad ones" mentioned in this parable are the scaleless catfish forbidden in Scripture and therefore not even offered for sale (v. 48). With this in mind, let us consider this question: Does my grandson Wesley's fearful surprise uncomfortably mirror our own response to the "bad ones" as we participate in the Kingdom's dragnet?

# 23 WHO'S GOOD AND WHAT'S BAD

I n Paul's first epistle to the Corinthians (which was actually a second letter, clearly written following a previous letter), we find a familiar scenario. Paul must spend six chapters defending his ministry and addressing blatant and overt problems in the Corinthian church. Then he must spend an additional five chapters (beginning with chapter 7) answering nagging and specific questions the Corinthians had sent to him. It thus takes eleven entire chapters, or more than half the letter, before Paul can write, "Now concerning spiritual matters..." (1 Cor.12:1).[104]

There is an implied sigh at this juncture, as though the great apostle is saying, "Now I can finally talk to you about the truly spiritual issues that are on my heart!" Every pastor and church leader is all too familiar with this scenario!

## The 'Good' vs. the 'Bad'

Jesus' choice of the dragnet comparison at the end of His set discourse on the Kingdom of God also has this significance. Although Jesus points to an inclusive world view of our task in all seven parables, His final comparison is the most startling. Galileans knew the precise image of the dragnet being dragged to shore so its contents could be spilled on the beach. It was an awesome and occasionally frightening perspective. They never knew what to expect. In some cases, like Wesley's experience, they probably dumped the net and ran!

Modern seining drops a huge circular net into the ocean depths. After a proper waiting period, a cord is eventually pulled that draws the bottom of the net together to form a huge basket. A crane-like device on the boat then hoists the net to the ship deck. And when the bottom is again pulled open and the contents of the net are dumped out, the deck literally slithers with a catch that includes both valuable and frightening things — sometimes even dead bodies!

Jesus' parable describes fishermen who cast the dragnet into the sea and then *"...gathered some of every kind, which, when it was full, they drew to shore; and they sat down and gathered the GOOD into vessels, but threw the bad away"* (vv. 47,48). Robert Capon believes that the Greek word for "good" needs careful examination.

> The words, "the good" and "the bad," however, are much more dubious translations. *Kalós in Greek does indeed mean "good," but with overtones of "beautiful," "fine," or "fair"*; it is *not as narrowly moralistic* as the other common Greek word for "good" (*agathós*). Jesus, for example, calls himself "the good shepherd" (*ho poimén ho kalós*), implying, presumably, that *he is something more than just an ethical shepherd* — that he is, in fact, an *admirable* one, even an extravagantly beneficent one. Still, *kalós* and *agathós* are often used more or less interchangeably for both moral and aesthetic (or utilitarian) goodness, so I want to put only a blunt, rather than a fine point on the distinction.[105]

I believe the distinction is important. Jesus speaks of the good here as *useful and fair*, not somehow moralistically pure or righteous.

Again, in a longer quote from *The Parables of the Kingdom*, Capon discusses the word Jesus used for "bad" — *saprós*.

*Saprós*, though, is another matter. Like most languages, Greek bears witness to the wretched state of human nature by having *more words for badness than for goodness*. *Kakós* is perhaps the most common word for "bad." But there are plenty of others: there is *ponérós*, "evil"; *ánomas*, "lawless"; *óthesmos*, "unsettled"; *phaulos*, "worthless"; and there is, of course, *saprós*; rotten, putrid, corrupt, worthless, useless." *Saprós* appears in five passages, four of which show its obvious suitability for use as the ugly opposite of *kalós*. Consider, for example, Matthew 7:17 (which displays along with the opposition of *kalós* and *saprós*, some other twists and turns of the Greek "good/evil" vocabulary): *"So every good [agathón] tree bringeth forth good [kalós] fruit; but a corrupt [saprós] tree bringeth forth evil [ponéros] fruit"* (KJV). Or for an even clearer illustration of the opposition of *kalós* and *saprós*, consider Matthew 12:33: *"Either make the tree good [kalón]; or else make the tree corrupt [saprón] and his fruit corrupt [saprón]"* (KJV). (The remaining passages, by the way, are Luke 6:43, parallel to Matt. 12:33, and Eph. 4:29, where *saprós* is contrasted with *agathós*.)[106]

The point must be obvious: The good and bad are evaluations of the fisherman based on what kind of catch he is pursuing. The fish (or other creeping things) are certainly not the ones to judge. In very clear language, Jesus explains who *will* serve in that role:

> "So it will be at the end of the age. The angels will come forth, separate the wicked from among the just,
>
> "and cast them into the furnace of fire. There will be wailing and gnashing of teeth."

**Matthew 13:49,50**

Perhaps the above discussion appears pedantic and even unnecessary. Quite the contrary! This era of the Kingdom is to be a net-dragging experience, *not* a time for division and judgment. The fisherman alone decides what is to be kept or thrown away.

Of course, there is no doubt about the destruction that eventually comes to those who thumb their noses at the reconciliation God has offered. Someone said, "Hell is the only option for people who are finally recalcitrant." But understand this well: No man ever goes to hell because of a poor track record, any more than a person goes to Heaven because of a *good* track record!

## The Right Attitude
## For Kingdom Preparation

This final parable is about our activity and our attitude during the era of Kingdom preparation. One often-quoted author on this parable writes: "The church, in short, has a role to play *only here and now; so if it wants a role model for its operations, it should imitate the Kingdom's present, nonjudgmental way of doing business, not its final one.*"[107] In other words, the church (as well as individual believers) should definitely not attempt to do the kind of sorting out in this world that has been clearly placed at the end of the age according to Kingdom purpose.

This calls for radical freedom and inclusiveness in our work as Kingdom seed. The work could not even be attempted without understanding a word that Jesus used several times in these seven parables — the word "understand." Nowhere was this word used in a more important context than in His concluding question to the disciples: "Have you *understood* all these things?" Although repetitious, we must reiterate that the word "understood" here (*suniemi*) means *to bring* or *to set together* — thus, *to unite our perception*.

For example, our clarity on the sacrifice and resulting reconciliation offered through the death, burial, and resurrection of Jesus Christ is more than doctrine. It is the foundation from which we as Kingdom sons and daughters operate!

There is no more succinct or clear instruction concerning our assignment than Second Corinthians 5:18-21:

Now all things are of God, who has reconciled us to Himself through Jesus Christ, and has given us the ministry of reconciliation,

that is, that God was in Christ reconciling the world to Himself, not imputing their trespasses to them, and has committed to us the word of reconciliation.

Now then, we are ambassadors for Christ, as though God were pleading through us: we implore you on Christ's behalf, be reconciled to God.

For He made Him who knew no sin to be sin for us, that we might become the righteousness of God in Him.

*Do we see humanity as not having their sins imputed unto them?* Do we accept the truth that God has been reconciled to the world through the offering of Jesus Christ? Do we see ourselves as ambassadors for Christ, pleading and imploring the world to be reconciled to God as He has been reconciled to them? We have an incredibly positive task, based entirely on Christ's unspeakable sacrifice and God's *amazing grace*.

## Our Message of Reconciliation
## To the World

Second Corinthians 5:18 says, *"Now all things are of God, who has reconciled us to Himself through Jesus Christ...."* Don't ever ask the average believer to explain the truth that once and for all, Jesus Christ was the accepted offering for sin — past, present, and future. That offering is unrepeatable; as in Moses' time, the rock may be struck only once. Jesus has already paid the price, for He was smitten and bruised for our transgressions.

It seems to me that evangelicals around the world should be erecting banners on every main street of the world that proclaim, *"God isn't mad at you any longer!"* Instead, people make a chronicle of their past sins — generally the ones they're less likely to commit at the present — believing that tears of sorrow are true signs of repentance.

But all transgression or trespass of the Law is sin. Sin is knowing to do right and not doing it. Everything not of faith is sin. And, finally, sin is to fall short of the glory of God. *Did you get that?* Even though you know Jesus, do you at all meet that high standard? *I don't think so!*

It has been said, "We're not going to be judged by what we were before the net caught us; the standards for the judgment are the divine Fisherman's standards." We all know John 3:16, but are we equally clear on the next two verses?

> **"For God did not send His Son into the world condemn the world, but that the world through Him might be saved.**
> **"He who believes in Him is not condemned; but he who does not believe is condemned already, because he has not believed in the name of the only begotten Son of God."**

This is to be our message, not only to the "good" but also to the "bad" brought in by the divine dragnet: "God isn't condemning you; He isn't mad at you. In fact, He has already sent His only Son to reconcile you to Himself!"

# 24 'NET DRAW-ERS'

W e often say, "Beauty is in the eye of the beholder." That is certainly true in God's case, for He always sees the world through the image of the finished, completed work of Calvary.

Satan overplayed his hand at Calvary. He thought that killing Jesus was a victory and that it would be the end. And it really was the end — the end of sin, the end of separation, the end of condemnation, the end of fear, the end of hopelessness. Thank God, we are not judged by our performance, but by Jesus Christ's performance — by what He accomplished on that Cross!

Now, of course, if a man wishes to argue with God's gracious plan of forgiveness, he can. As one writer observes "Hell is a courtesy for those who insist they want no part of God's forgiveness."[108] That same writer continues:

> Everyone who comes before the Judge has already been reconciled by the dying and rising of the Judge. The only sentence to be pronounced as far as the judge is concerned is a sentence to life and life abundantly.[109]

## The Kingdom Attitude:
## Inclusive, Not Exclusive

The picturesque drama involving a dragnet must be a convicting revelation to the true believer and the honest and caring church. It explains our task, speaks to our philosophy and method, and challenges the deepest core of our being — *our attitude.*

William Barclay writes, "The Christian Church must be open to all, and that, like the dragnet...it is bound to be a mixture."[110] There seems to be a subtle tendency among those found by the divine dragnet to dislike or judge other types of equally favored ones who have also been caught in God's provision. Perhaps it *is* possible to "love souls, yet hate *people.*"

But we must never forget the spirit displayed by the Pharisee whom Jesus quoted as saying, *"...'God, I thank You that I am not like other men — extortioners, unjust, adulterers, or even as this tax collector"* (Luke 18:11).

Robert Farrar Capon, to whom I owe a phenomenal debt on the subject of the dragnet, gives the following conclusive statement. Check your spirit as you read it. It is, after all, ultimately a statement about attitude.

Sinners are the church's *business*, for God's sake. Literally. Let the scribes and the Pharisees — the phony-baloney, super-righteous, unforgiving scorekeepers who delight in getting everybody's number — take care of any judging that they want to: *judgment now* is their cup of tea, and they can poison themselves all they want with it. But let the church — which works for somebody who delights in getting everybody's *name* — stay a million miles away from it. We are supposed to represent a Lord who came not to judge the world but to save it. Our business should be simply to keep everybody in the net of his kingdom until we reach the farther shore. Sorting is strictly his department, not ours.[111]

The Kingdom of Heaven is like a dragnet cast into the sea. We can choose to spend our time concentrating on the ultimate beachside separation of "the good versus the bad." But we can also choose to fulfill our call as influencers of this age for God's Kingdom. We do that by participating in the endtime task of *drawing in the net* — maintaining the subtle pressure and compassion that keeps the world within our reach.

This is the true purpose of the Kingdom in this present age, for the scope and provision of Christ's sacrifice is limitless. Indeed, it encompasses the *world*.

# In Conclusion – Remembering

Jesus said to them, "Have you understood all these things?" They said to Him, "Yes, Lord."

Then He said to them, "Therefore every scribe instructed concerning the kingdom of heaven is like a householder who brings out of his treasure things new and old."

Matthew 13:51,52

Jesus asked, "Are you starting to get a handle on all this?" They answered, "Yes."

He said, "Then you see how every student well-trained in God's kingdom is like the owner of a general store who can put his hands on anything you need, old or new, exactly when you need it."

Matthew 13:51,52

*The Message*
Eugene Peterson

# STRUCTURE OF MATTHEW 'THE KING AND HIS KINGDOM'[112]

PRELUDE: The Coming of the King *(chapters 1-2)*

I.   The Presentation of the King *(chapters 3-4)* and of His Kingdom *(chapters 5-7)*

> *7:28 (KJV) And it came to pass, when Jesus had ended these sayings, the people were astonished at his doctrine.*

II.  The Authority of the King *(chapters 8-9)* and of His Kingdom *(chapters 10-11)*

> *11:1 (KJV) And it came to pass, when Jesus had made an end of commanding his twelve disciples, he departed thence to teach and to preach in their cities.*

III. Opposition to the King *(chapters 12-13)* and to His Kingdom *(chapters 14-16:12)*

*13:53 (KJV) And it came to pass, that when Jesus had finished these parables, he departed thence.*

IV. Private Recognition of the King *(chapter 16:13-chapter 17)* and of His Kingdom *(chapter 18)*

> *19:1 (KJV) And it came to pass, that when Jesus had finished these sayings, he departed from Galilee, and came into the coasts of Judaea beyond Jordan.*

V. Public Rejection of the King *(chapters 19-22)* and of His Kingdom *(chapter 23)*

> *23:37-24:1 (KJV) O Jerusalem, Jerusalem, thou that killest the prophets, and stonest them which are sent unto thee, how often would I have gathered thy children together, even as a hen gathereth her chickens under her wings, and ye would not! Behold, your house is left unto you desolate. For I say unto you, Ye shall not see me henceforth, till ye shall say, Blessed is he that cometh in the name of the Lord. And Jesus went out, and departed from the temple: and his disciples came to him for to shew him the buildings of the temple.*

VI. The Great Prophecy of the Kingdom *(chapters 24-25)*

> *26:1-2 (KJV) And it came to pass, when Jesus had finished all these sayings, he said unto his disciples, Ye know that after two days is the feast of the passover, and the Son of man is betrayed to be crucified.*

VII. The Great Passion of the King *(chapters 26-27)*

FINALE: The Triumph of the King and His Kingdom *(chapter 28)*

# ENDNOTES

## Author's Preface

[1]Quoted by the Reverend Donald Gibbs in a sermon at Westminster Chapel in London, England on Sunday, August 12, 2001.

## Chapter One

[2]The author is well aware of the many theories of Gospel composition and even that of suggested copying from one writer to another. Recent scholarship has been forced to give Matthew a much earlier dating than previously recognized. We stand on this assertion, aware of some scholarly contempt, i.e., "The Brother of Jesus," *Time Magazine*, November 4, 2002, pp. 70-73.

[3]In this and all other quoted material, italics are added by this author for purposes of specific emphasis.

[4]Matthew 13:53 (*NIV*): *"When Jesus had finished these parables, he moved on from there."*

[5]Dean Alford as quoted by G. Campbell Morgan in *The Gospel According to Matthew* (New York: Fleming H. Revell Company, 1929), p. 139.

[6]Morgan, op. cit., p. 139.

[7]John Bright, *The Kingdom of God* (Nashville: Abingdon Press, 1981), p. 252.

[8]Donald B. Kraybill, *The Upside-Down Kingdom*, Revised Edition (Scottsdale, PA: Herald Press, 1990).

[9]G. E. Ladd, *Jesus and the Kingdom* (1966, p. 303), as quoted in *The Zondervan Pictorial Encyclopedia of the Bible, Vol. 3, H-L* (Grand Rapids, Michigan: Zondervan, 1976).

[10]Bright, op. cit., p. 252.

[11]Ibid.

[12]Morgan, op. cit., p. 179.

[13]Kraybill, op. cit., p. 61.

[14]Alexander Maclaren, *Expositions of Holy Scripture, St. Matthew Chap. 9-28* (Grand Rapids, Michigan: Wm. B. Eerdmans Publishing Co., 1932), p. 238.

[15]Morgan, op. cit., p. 147.

## Chapter Two

[16]Morgan, op. cit., p. 179.

[17]Matthew's parallel to Luke 11:20 is Matthew 12:28, where "finger of God" becomes "Spirit of God."

## Chapter Three

[18]Brad H. Young, *Jesus and His Jewish Parables* (Mahwah, New Jersey: Paulist Press, 1989), back cover.

[19]Matthew structured his Gospel around Christ's discourses, followed by His departures: the Sermon on the Mount (7:28); the Commission of the Twelve (11:1); the Parables of the Kingdom (13:53); on Greatness and Forgiveness (19:1); the Woes on the Scribes and Pharisees (23:39-24:1); and the Olivet Discourse (26:1,2). Please refer to the outline entitled "Structure of Matthew: The King and His Kingdom" on page 175.

[20]Morgan, op. cit., p. 179.

## Chapter Four

[21]Eugene H. Peterson, *The Message* (Colorado Springs: NavPress, 1993), p. 44.

[22]Acts 13:36: *"For David, after he had served his own generation by the will of God, fell asleep, was buried with his fathers, and saw corruption."*

## Chapter Five

[23]Quote in verse 35 is from Psalm 78:2.

[24]Robert Farrar Capon, *The Parables of the Kingdom* (Grand Rapids, Michigan: Wm. B. Eerdmans Publishing Co., 1985), p. 10.

[25]Bob E. Patterson, *Discovering Matthew, The Guideposts Home Bible Study Program* (Carmel, New York: Guideposts, 1985), p. 83.

[26]Quote is from Isaiah 6:9,10.

[27]Peterson, pp. 41-42.

[28]G. K. Chesterton, as quoted by Robert Farrar Capon, op. cit., p. 8.

## Chapter Six

[29]Morgan, op. cit., p. 147.

[30]Vincent, *Word Studies of the New Testament, Vol. I* (Mclean, Virginia: MacDonald Publishing Co., n.d.), p. 79.

[31]Fritz Kienecker and Cleon Rogers, *Linguistic Keys to the Greek New Testament* (Grand Rapids, Michigan: Regency Reference Library, Zondervan Publishing House, 1980), p. 39.

[32]Archibald Thomas Robertson, *Word Pictures in the New Testament, Vol. I* (Nashville: Broadman Press, 1930), p. 106.

## Chapter Eight

[33]According to the writings of Josephus, Galilee in the time of Jesus had approximately 204 cities and villages, each with no fewer than 15,000 persons.

[34]Vincent, op. cit., p. 79.

[35]Morgan, op. cit., p. 147.

## Chapter Nine

[36]In fact, not one of the twelve stood fast initially, but only one was ultimately lost. The rest were afterward restored, commissioned, and empowered.

[37]Quoted from Isaiah 61:1,2.

## Chapter Ten

[38]*The Compact Edition of the English Dictionary* (Oxford: Oxford University Press, 1971), p. 2723.

[39]Capon, op. cit., p. 15.

[40]Morgan, op. cit., p. 149.

[41]Ibid.

[42]Ladd, op. cit.

## Chapter Eleven

[43]William Barclay, *The Daily Study Bible, The Gospel of Matthew, Vol. 2* (Philadelphia: The Westminster Press, 1950), p. 82.

## Chapter Twelve

[44]Morgan, op. cit., p. 176.

## Chapter Thirteen

[45]Kraybill, op. cit., pp. 170-171.

[46]Ibid., p. 171.

[47]Maclaren, op. cit., p. 238.

[48]Philip B. Payne, "Jesus' Implicit Claim to Deity in His Parables," *Trinity Journal*, 1981, pp. 3-23.

[49]Young, op. cit.
[50]Ray Stedman, "The Case of the Mysterious Harvest," sermon preached at Peninsula Bible Church in Palo Alto, California (Palo Alto: Discovery Publishing, May 23, 1971), p. 16.
[51]Maclaren, op. cit. p. 236.
[52]Morgan, op. cit., p. 152.
[53]Maclaren, op. cit., p. 235.
[54]Morgan, op. cit., p. 152.
[55]Stedman, op. cit., p. 16.

## Chapter Fourteen

[56]Maclaren, op. cit., p. 236.
[57]Barclay, op. cit. pp. 82-83.
[58]Ibid., p. 83.
[59]Maclaren, op. cit., p. 242.
[60]Ibid., p. 243.
[61]Ibid., p. 242.
[62]Ibid., p. 243.
[63]Ibid.

## Chapter Fifteen

[64]Morgan, op. cit., p. 178.
[65]Ibid., p. 152.
[66]Ibid.
[67]Ibid., p. 153.
[68]Maltbie D. Babcock, 1901.
[69]Morgan, op. cit., 149.
[70]Ibid., 153.
[71]Kraybill, op. cit., p. 271.
[72]Ibid.
[73]Ibid.

## Chapter Sixteen

[74]Jacques Dupont as quoted in *The Expositors Bible Commentary*, op. cit., p. 318.
[75]Barclay, op. cit., p. 88.
[76]Ibid., p. 85.
[77]Patterson, op. cit., p. 86.
[78]Ibid.
[79]*The Expositors Bible Commentary*, op. cit., p. 318.
[80]Morgan, op. cit., p. 155.
[81]*Guideposts*, op. cit., p. 87.

⁸²Barclay, op. cit., p. 88.
⁸³Capon, op. cit., p. 118.
⁸⁴Ibid., pp. 118-119.
⁸⁵Stedman, op. cit., p. 22.

## Chapter Seventeen

⁸⁶Barclay, op. cit., p. 93.
⁸⁷Andre Crouch, "My Tribute," Lexicon Music, 1971.

## Chapter Eighteen

⁸⁸Randolph O. Yeager, *The Renaissance New Testament, Vol. Two* (Bowling Green, Kentucky: Renaissance Press, 1977), p. 400.
⁸⁹Capon, op. cit., p. 138.

## Chapter Nineteen

⁹⁰Joseph Conrad, as quoted by Linda Gomez, "Eight Great Buried Treasures," *Life* Magazine, March 1987, p. 29.
⁹¹Capon, op. cit., p. 137.
⁹²*See* also Malachi 3:17.
⁹³Capon, op. cit., p. 142.

## Chapter Twenty

⁹⁴J. B. Phillips, *The New Testament in Modern English* (New York: The MacMillan Co., 1962), p. 364.

## Chapter Twenty-One

⁹⁵It wasn't until the thirteenth century that Cardinal Hugo changed the New Testament manuscript into chapters and not until 1545 that Robert Stephanus divided the chapters into verses.
⁹⁶Barclay, op. cit., p. 102.
⁹⁷Ibid.
⁹⁸*"But blessed are your eyes, for they see: and your ears, for they hear. For verily I say unto you, That many prophets and righteous men have desired to see those things which ye see, and have not seen them; and to hear those things which ye hear, and have not heard them"* (Matt. 13:16,17).

## Chapter Twenty-Two

⁹⁹Capon, op. cit., p. 148.
¹⁰⁰Mendel Nun, "The Kingdom of Heaven Is Like a Seine," *Jerusalem Perspective*, http://www.jerusalemperspective.com/articles/DisplayArticle.asp?ID=1452

[101]Ibid.

[102]Ibid.

[103]Capon, op. cit., p. 151.

## Chapter Twenty-Three

[104]Obviously, most translations read "concerning spiritual *gifts*," but the word "gifts" is not in the original manuscripts and is supplied by the translator.

[105]Capon, op. cit., p. 154.

[106]Capon, op. cit., p. 154-155.

[107]Capon, op. cit., p. 151.

## Chapter Twenty-Four

[108]Capon, op. cit., p. 157.

[109]Ibid., p. 156.

[110]Barclay, op. cit., p. 100.

[111]Capon, op. cit., p. 158.

## Structure of Matthew

[112]Adapted from W. Graham Scroggie, *A Guide to the Gospels* (Old Tappan, New Jersey: Fleming H. Revell, undated), pp. 255-256.

# OTHER BOOKS BY RICK C. HOWARD

*Songs From Life* (hardback)

*Strategy for Triumph: A Christian Perspective on Problems*

*The Finding Times of God*

*The Judgment Seat of Christ*

*The Judgment Seat of Christ* (Spanish)

*The Lost Formula of the Early Church* (hardback)

*Seven Biblical Steps to Personal Renewal*

*This Was Your Life* (co-authored with Jamie Lash)

*Restoring Restorers*

# ABOUT THE AUTHOR

Rick C. Howard is a pastor whose pulpit is the world. He is the author of fourteen books, including the best-selling *The Judgment Seat of Christ*, now translated in Chinese, Spanish, Bulgarian, Japanese, and French. Two of his books are translated in more than thirty languages.

Rick is a frequent speaker at conferences and has ministered in more than eighty nations. He served on the faculty of a major Christian college for fourteen years and is presently adjunct faculty of Asia Pacific Theological Seminary. Rick's pastorate in the San Francisco Bay Area lasted thirty years. He is currently the Missions Pastor of the same church and remains committed to the message of restoration and reconciliation.

# Naioth Sound and Publishing

2995 Woodside Road, Suite 400
Woodside, California 94062
Toll free: 1-800-726-3127
Fax: 1-650-368-0790


Discounts for volume amounts:
40% discount for bookstores
50% discount for churches
60% discount for distributors